the [Visual] Guide to Kindergarten

Thinking Kids™
An imprint of Carson-Dellosa Publishing LLC
P.O. Box 35665
Greensboro, NC 27425 USA

Thinking Kids™
An imprint of Carson-Dellosa Publishing LLC
P.O. Box 35665
Greensboro, NC 27425 USA

ISBN 978-1-4838-2681-3

Infographics and Learning Activities

Spiders 6
Think and Solve; Match It: Piece It Together: Spiders or Insects? 8

All About Apples 12
Think and Solve; Label It; Make a Graph 14

Rocks That Rock! 16
Think and Solve; Explore Your World 17

Desert Tracks 18
Think and Solve; Match It; Read About It: Right on Track; Try It Yourself 20

Float or Sink? 22
Think and Solve; Piece It Together: Did It Sink or Float? 24

Waste Not! 28
Think and Solve; Match It; Log It 30

Meet the Emperor 32
True or False?; Classify It; Read About It: Waiting for Baby; Draw and Write 34

The American Flag 36
Think and Solve; Color It; Do the Math; Write About It 38

10 Reasons to Be a Farmer 40
Think and Solve; Write About It; Read About It: Farmer Tucker's Busy Day;
Piece It Together: Farmer Tucker's Day 41

Foods From American Indians 46
Think and Solve; Identify It; Make a Plan 48

It All Makes Sense 50
Make Idea Webs; Guess It 52

Going, Going, Gone 54
Do the Math; Try It Yourself 55

All About Pumpkins 56
Think and Solve; Finish the Pattern; Do the Math 58

What to See in Washington, DC 60
Think and Solve; Read About It: Chief Tecumseh; Try It Yourself; Schedule It 62

The Mighty T. Rex 64
Think and Solve; Describe It; Piece It Together: T. Rex 66

From Cow to Cone 70
Think and Solve; Make a Process Chart 72

What's Out There? 74
Think and Solve; Match It; Piece It Together: What Does It Orbit? 76

Country Life and City Life 80
Think and Solve; Classify It; Compare and Contrast 82

Special Days Around the World 84
Label It; Make a Chart 86

Pretty Patterns 88
Classify It; Show It; Finish the Pattern; Color It 90

More Than One 92
Do the Math; Match It; Piece It Together: How Many Babies? 94

Neat Seeds 98
Think and Solve; Sequence It 99

Money Matters 100
Think and Solve; Do the Math; Explore Your World 102

A Way to Go 104
Do the Math; Make a Bar Graph 105

Carved in Stone 106
Think and Solve; Match It; Label It; Imagine It 108

The Lovely Ladybug 110
Think and Solve; Do the Math; Label It 112

Edison's Amazing Inventions 114
Think and Solve; Match It; Make an Idea Web; Imagine It 116

Oceans Alive 118
Think and Solve; Read About It: Finding Food in the Forest; Piece It Together:
A Forest Food Chain 120

The Liberty Bell 124
Think and Solve; Explore Your World; Write About It 126

Toys From Around the World 128
Think and Solve; Sequence It; Try It Yourself 130

Happy Birthday! 132
Think and Solve; Do the Math 133

Looking for Freedom 134
Think and Solve; Match It; Write About It 136

Know Your Snow! 138
Piece It Together: Build a Snowman 139

The Inuit People 142
Think and Solve; Match It; Label It 144

Crossing the Globe 146
Think and Solve; Match It; Use a Calendar 148

A Crop of Corn 150
Think and Solve; Explore Your World; Log It 152

Professor Carver's Peanuts 154
Think and Solve; Describe It; Collect Data; Make a Picture Chart 156

Tugboats on the Move 158
Think and Solve; Match It 159

Super Teeth 160
Think and Solve; Show It; Log It; Color It 162

Fruit or Veggie? 164
Think and Solve; Rank It; Piece It Together: Fruit or Vegetable? 166

Grown-Up Jobs 170
Think and Solve; Do the Math; Match It; Imagine It 172

Video Games: The Good and the Bad 174
Log It; Make a Pie Chart; Think and Solve 176

Answer Key 178

Spiders

There are about 40,000 different kinds of spiders in the world!

Spiders are found all over the world except for Antarctica.

Some spiders spin sticky webs to catch their food. Many spiders sit in the center of their webs and wait for insects to get stuck inside.

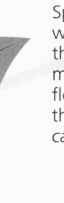

Spiders often blend in with the things around them. Their bodies may look like tree bark, flowers, or other natural things. This is called *camouflage*.

Spiders are not insects. They are *arachnids*. Arachnids have eight legs and do not have antennae. Scorpions and ticks are arachnids, too.

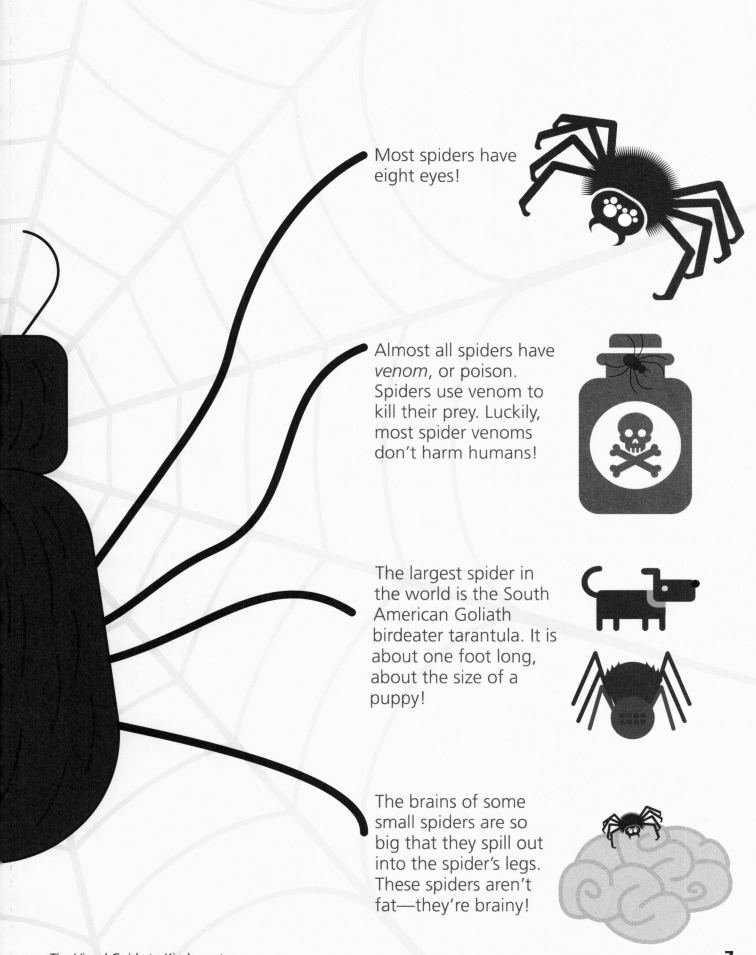

Most spiders have eight eyes!

Almost all spiders have *venom*, or poison. Spiders use venom to kill their prey. Luckily, most spider venoms don't harm humans!

The largest spider in the world is the South American Goliath birdeater tarantula. It is about one foot long, about the size of a puppy!

The brains of some small spiders are so big that they spill out into the spider's legs. These spiders aren't fat—they're brainy!

Think and Solve

Study the infographic. Answer the questions.

1. Most spider venom is harmful to humans.

    True   **False**

2. Spiders have _____ legs.

3. What is one way spiders can catch food? _____

_____

Match It

Draw a line to match each spider with its description.

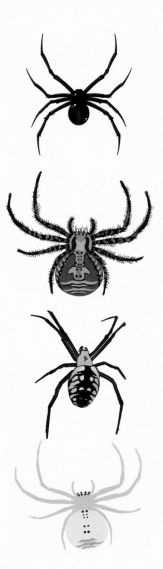

Garden Spider
This spider has a yellow and
black pattern on its body and legs.

Black Widow
The female has a red hourglass
shape on her black belly.

Giant Crab Spider
This large, light brown
spider has long legs.

Green Crab Spider
This light green spider
has long front legs.

Piece It Together

Cut out the facts about spiders and insects. Glue or tape them under the correct headings on page 11.

It takes a spider about an hour to build a web.

Bees, butterflies, ants, and beetles are all insects.

Some insects are helpful. Others are seen as pests.

Spiders have bodies with two sections.

Spiders spin silk that is very strong.

Insects have bodies with three sections.

There are more than one million types of insects in the world.

Spiders do not have very good eyesight.

Spiders or Insects?

Spiders

Insects

All About Apples

Apples are crunchy fruits that grow on trees. They can be sweet or tart. What is your favorite way to eat apples?

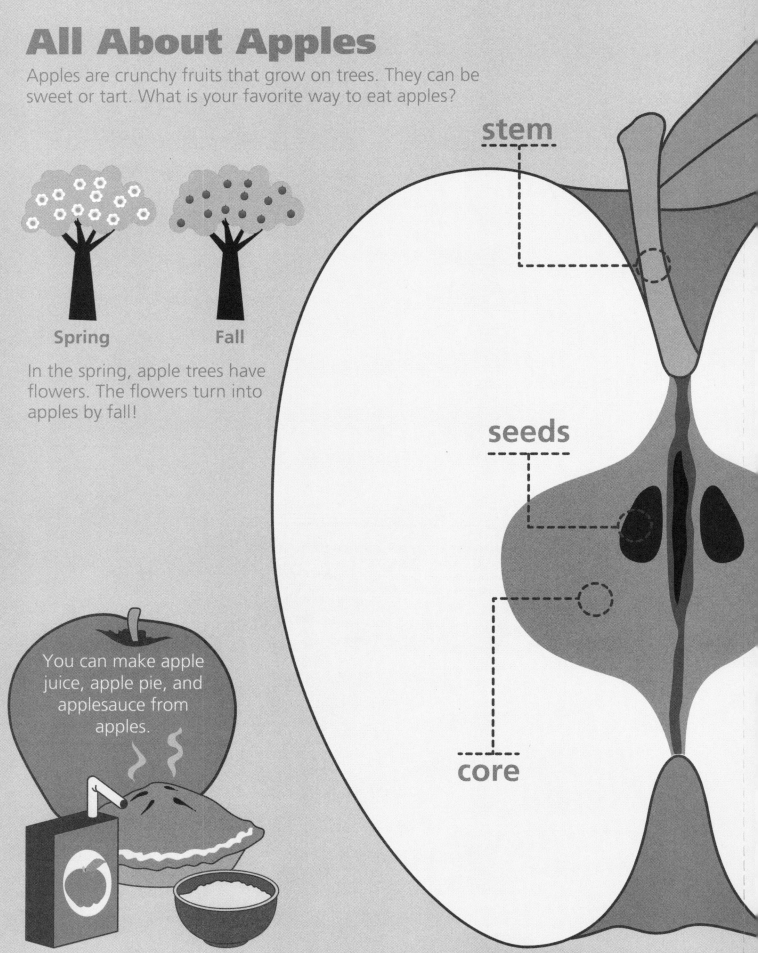

Spring

Fall

In the spring, apple trees have flowers. The flowers turn into apples by fall!

You can make apple juice, apple pie, and applesauce from apples.

stem

seeds

core

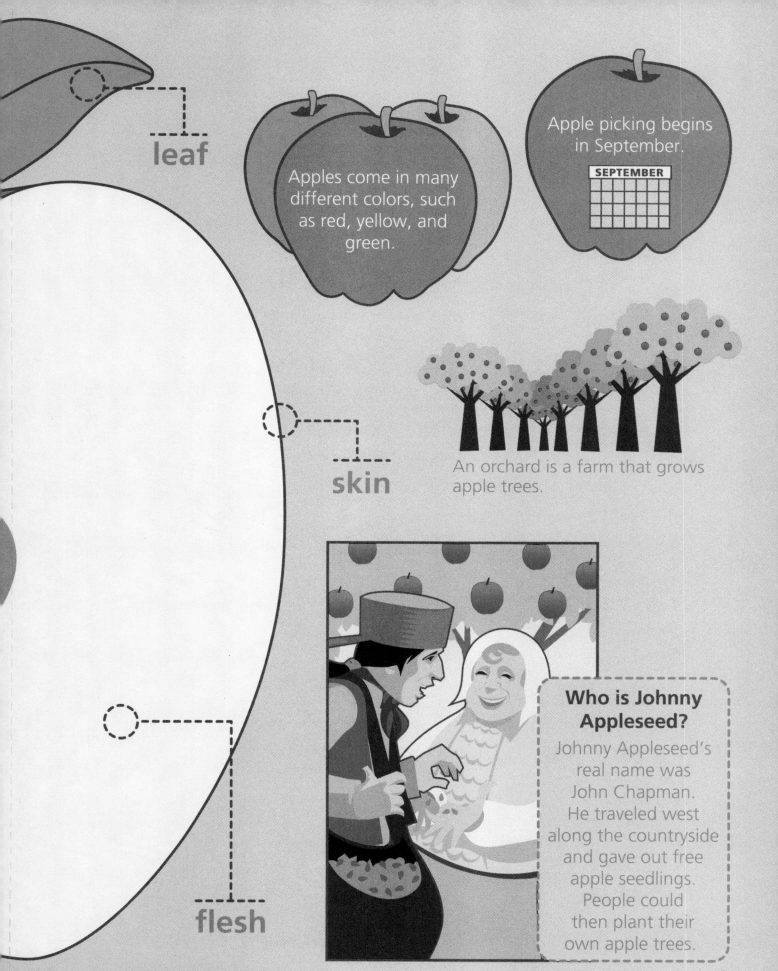

leaf

Apples come in many different colors, such as red, yellow, and green.

Apple picking begins in September.

SEPTEMBER

skin

An orchard is a farm that grows apple trees.

flesh

Who is Johnny Appleseed?

Johnny Appleseed's real name was John Chapman. He traveled west along the countryside and gave out free apple seedlings. People could then plant their own apple trees.

Think and Solve

Study the infographic. Answer the questions.

1. When do apple trees have flowers?

    A. winter

    B. spring

    C. summer

    D. fall

2. An apple farm is called an _____ .

3. List three colors that apples can be.

    _____   _____   _____

Label It

Use the words to label each part of the apple.

core

flesh

leaf

seeds

skin

stem

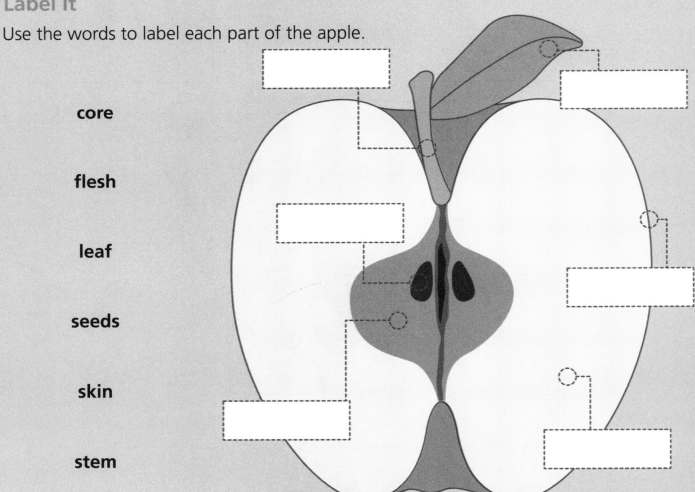

Make a Graph

Count the apples in each basket. Color the graph to show how many.
Basket A has been done for you.

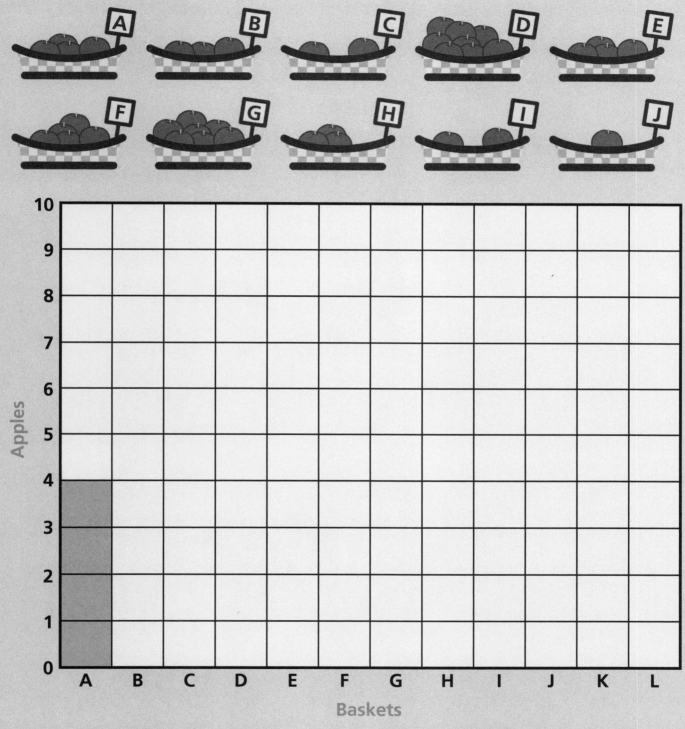

Now, draw apples in Baskets K and L.
Add them to the graph.

Rocks That Rock!

Many kinds of rocks can be found on Earth. Rocks are made of minerals.
Rocks are fun to look for and collect.

Glow rocks

Glow rocks are fluorescent. These colorful rocks glow when you put them under a special kind of light.

Moon rocks

Moon rocks, also called *lunar rocks*, are from the moon! Astronauts bring back moon rocks to study more about the moon. They are mostly gray. But they can have bits of brown, green, red, or yellow glass in them.

Geodes

Geodes are rocks that are filled with a surprise. The rocks look dull and gray on the outside, but when you break one apart, there are beautiful crystals inside!

Pumice stones

Pumice stones are made by volcanoes. They have lots of small holes and are very light. Pumice stones will float in water.

Wishing rocks

Wishing rocks are stones with a line all the way around them. They can be big or small. When you find one of these special rocks, make a wish!

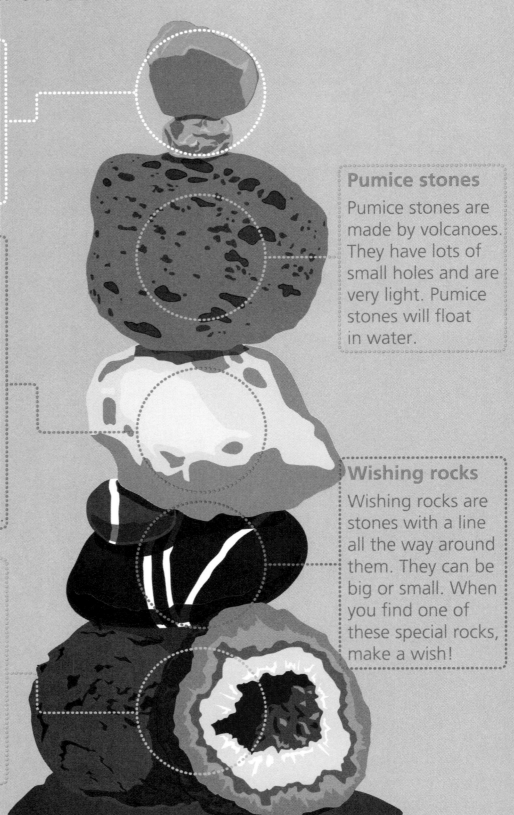

Think and Solve

Study the infographic. Answer the questions.

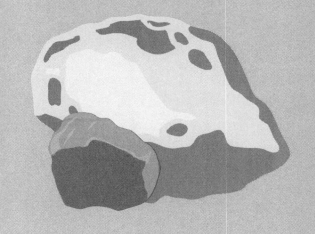

1. What are rocks made of?

    A. crystals

    B. geodes

    C. minerals

    D. stones

2. Pumice stones are made by _____.

3. True or false? Some moon rocks have glass in them. _____

Explore Your World

Find eight rocks. Use the chart to tell about each rock. Circle words that describe the rock. Then, write an interesting fact about each rock.

	Color		Size		Shape		Facts
Rock 1	white gray	black other:_____	small	big	flat	round	
Rock 2	white gray	black other:_____	small	big	flat	round	
Rock 3	white gray	black other:_____	small	big	flat	round	
Rock 4	white gray	black other:_____	small	big	flat	round	
Rock 5	white gray	black other:_____	small	big	flat	round	
Rock 6	white gray	black other:_____	small	big	flat	round	
Rock 7	white gray	black other:_____	small	big	flat	round	
Rock 8	white gray	black other:_____	small	big	flat	round	

Desert Tracks

The desert is a hot and dry place. It is easy to find animal tracks in the desert because it does not rain very much. The tracks stay in place.

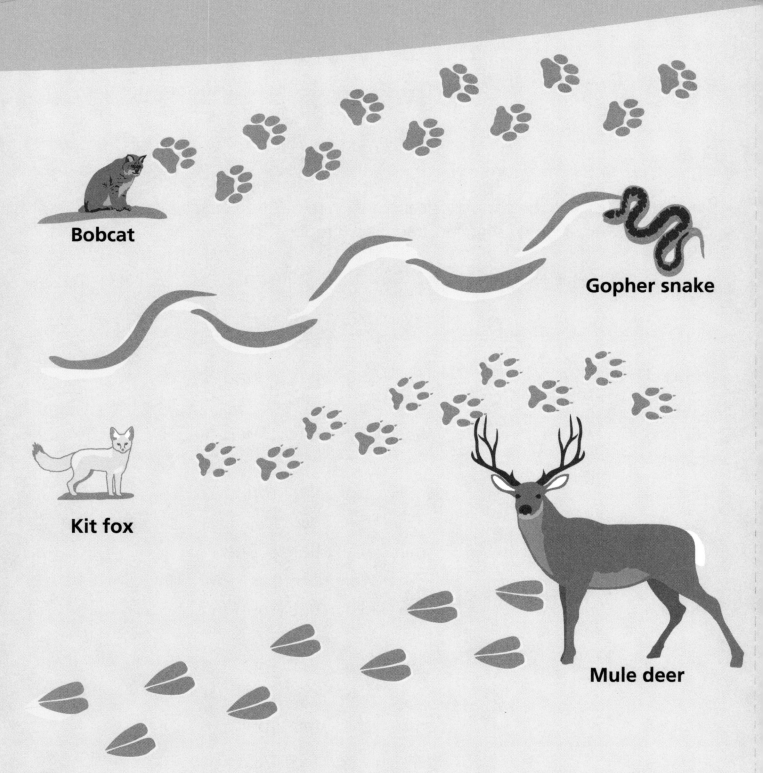

Bobcat

Gopher snake

Kit fox

Mule deer

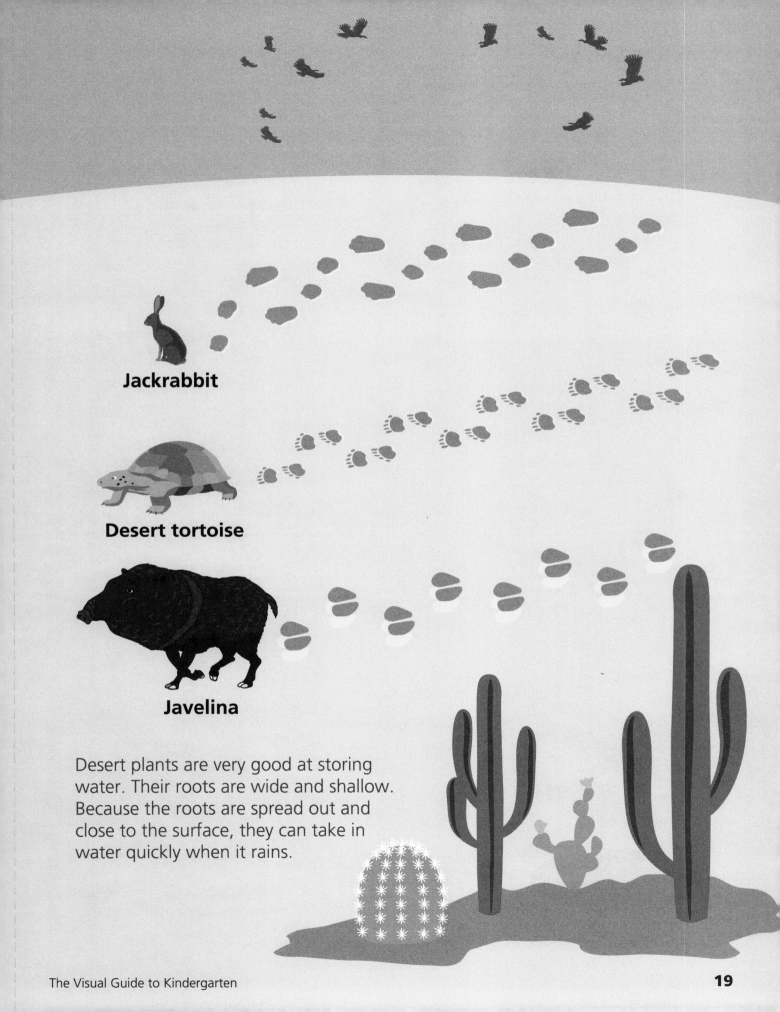

Jackrabbit

Desert tortoise

Javelina

Desert plants are very good at storing water. Their roots are wide and shallow. Because the roots are spread out and close to the surface, they can take in water quickly when it rains.

Think and Solve

Study the infographic. Answer the questions.

1. There are no plants in the desert.

   True   **False**

2. How many mule deer footprints are shown on the infographic? _____

3. Which animal looks most like a javelina?

   A. a sheep

   B. a cow

   C. a prairie dog

   D. a pig

Match It

Draw a line to match each animal with its tracks.

Read About It: Right on Track

TO FIND TRACKS IN NATURE, look in a place where animals gather. It might be where they eat or drink. Try looking at the bank of a creek or under a bird feeder. If you have trouble finding tracks, ask an adult to help you set out some food in the evening. Try seeds, nuts, or fruit and vegetable scraps. In the morning, check the spot. Do you see tracks around the place?

When you find animal tracks, make a drawing to help you remember what they looked like. Or, take a photograph of the tracks. When you get home, try to find out what type of animal made the tracks. Use a field guide from the library or have an adult help you look online.

Try It Yourself

Follow the directions for finding animal tracks. What kinds of tracks did you see? In the spaces below, draw two kinds of tracks you found. Write the date when you found each track, the name of the animal that made the tracks, and the name of the place where you found the tracks.

Date:_____ Date:_____

Animal: _____ Animal: _____

Place: _____ Place: _____

Float or Sink?

Will an object float in water, or sink? The answer depends on how *dense* the object is.

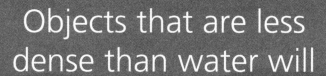

Objects that are less dense than water will

FLOAT

on the water.

Most rocks are dense. That means they are very solid. A small rock is about the same size as a small block of wood, but it weighs more. Rock is more solid than wood, so rock is denser than wood. Most rocks sink in water.

Why? The rind of the lemon is different. It has tiny air pockets in it that help the lemon float. The lime's rind is denser than the water, so it sinks.

Objects that are more dense than water will

SINK

under the water.

Most wood is not very dense. It has pockets of air that keep it from being solid. A small wood block is about the same size as a small rock, but it weighs less. Wood is less solid than rock, so wood is less dense than rock. Many kinds of wood float in water.

Think and Solve

Study the infographic. Answer the questions.

1. Objects float when they are _____ dense than water.

    A. more   **B.** less

2. A _____ will sink in water.

    A. lime   **B.** lemon

3. A stick floats. What do you know about the stick?

    A. It is very light.

    B. It is denser than water.

    C. It weighs more than water.

    D. It is less dense than water.

4. Draw one thing you think would sink in water.

5. Draw one thing you think would float in water.

Piece It Together

Look at the pictures. Ask an adult to help you find each item around the house. Then, think about each thing. Will it sink or float? Make a guess.

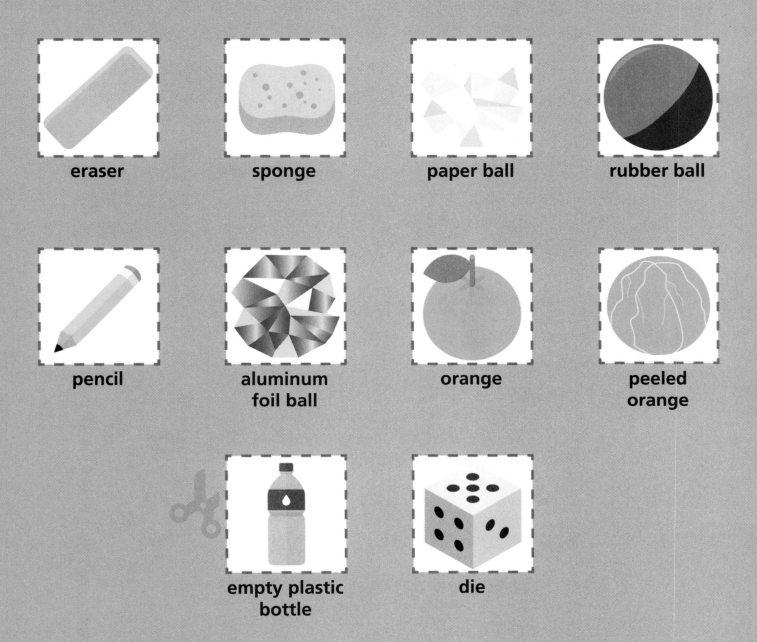

eraser

sponge

paper ball

rubber ball

pencil

aluminum foil ball

orange

peeled orange

empty plastic bottle

die

Next, fill a bucket with water. Cut apart the pictures. Test each item to see if it floats or sinks. Glue or tape each picture onto page 27. If it floats, put the picture at the top. If it sinks, put the picture on the bottom. Was your guess correct?

Did It Sink or Float?

Float

Sink

Waste Not!

This is a recycling symbol. Recycling means that old products can be made into new products.

Old plastic bottles can be turned into fabric for making new clothes, backpacks, or sleeping bags.

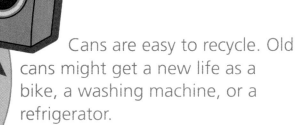

Cans are easy to recycle. Old cans might get a new life as a bike, a washing machine, or a refrigerator.

When you recycle an old cardboard box, it provides new material for making paper bags, cereal boxes, or even new cardboard boxes.

Recycled paper might get turned into tissues, paper towels, or napkins.

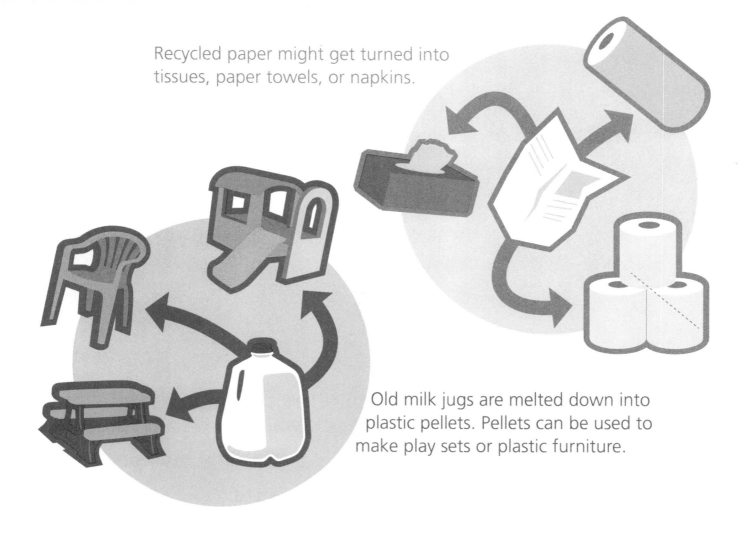

Old milk jugs are melted down into plastic pellets. Pellets can be used to make play sets or plastic furniture.

Did you know that kids can recycle, too?

You can make a puppet with a paper bag!

You can plant a seed in a plastic cup and then plant it in your garden!

Save baby food jars or other small jars. Use them to hold paints and brushes!

Swap with your friends! Trade old games, toys, and clothes you don't use anymore.

Think and Solve

Study the infographic. Answer the questions.

1. Metal cans might be recycled into a _____.

2. When you _____, old products can be made into new products.

3. Tell about one way kids can recycle.

_____

_____

_____

Match It

Draw a line to match recycled items with new items that can be made from recycled materials.

Log It

Keep track of what you recycle every day for a week. Make a tally mark (|) for each item you recycle. Write the total number of items at the end of each row. Then, answer the questions.

	= 1	|| = 2	||| = 3	|||| = 4	ⅢⅡ = 5

Item	Tally Marks	Total

How many items did you recycle in all? _____

About how many items did you recycle each day? _____

What item did you recycle most?_____

What item did you recycle least? _____

What item will you try to recycle more often? _____

Meet the Emperor

Emperor penguins DO...

- stand up to 4 feet tall!
- have colorful feathers around their necks and heads!
- live in Antarctica!
- huddle together to stay warm!
- dive deeper underwater than any other bird!

Emperor penguins DO NOT...

- stand alone! They live in colonies.
- eat pizza! They eat fish and krill.
- fly! They have flippers instead of wings.
- need to wear jackets! They have four layers of feathers and lots of fat to keep them warm.
- wait until spring to breed! They breed as soon as the ice gets thick enough to support their weight.

After laying an egg, the **female penguin** leaves. She goes on a long hunting trip across the ice to the sea. She may have to travel up to 50 miles. Her trip can last for two months! The female comes back carrying food for her new chick.

The **male penguin** is a good dad. When the mother goes away to find food, the dad will keep the egg warm. He does this by putting the egg under a flap above his feet. After about 65 days, the egg hatches.

The **baby chick** does not look like his parents. He has gray feathers. He makes a special sound so his parents can find and feed him. The chick will eat and grow a lot in his first year.

Chicks gather in groups called *crèches*. When summer comes, the ice breaks up. Then, the chicks can swim and find food on their own.

True or False?

Read each sentence. If it is true, circle *T*. If it is false, circle *F*.

1. Penguins are not good at diving underwater.   **T**   **F**

2. Penguins huddle together to keep warm.   **T**   **F**

3. Most penguins live alone.   **T**   **F**

4. Penguins are birds but do not fly.   **T**   **F**

5. Emperor penguins can be six feet tall!   **T**   **F**

6. The male penguin keeps the egg warm.   **T**   **F**

Classify It

Circle pictures of things found in Antarctica. Make an X on things not found there. If you need help, ask an adult to help you look in a book or online.

Read About It: Waiting for Baby

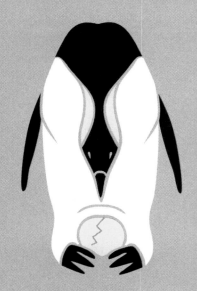

SAM IS GOING TO BE A FATHER. He has been waiting and waiting. He looks at the egg nestled on his feet. How much longer will it be? He is hungry. He misses Anna. She has been gone for months! Soon, she will be home with food for the new baby. Wait! What was that sound? Crrrr-ack!

Draw and Write

Write and draw an ending for the story.

_____

_____

_____

_____

_____

_____

The American Flag

The flag is a symbol of the United States of America.

Each star stands for one of the 50 states.

Each red or white stripe stands for one of the 13 colonies. The colonies were here before America became a country.

The last star that was added to the flag stands for the last state that was added to the country—Hawaii.

The flag is almost twice as long as it is tall.

Flag Nicknames

Old Glory

The Star-Spangled Banner

The The Red, White, and Blue
The Stars and Stripes

Flag Day

JUNE						
S	**M**	**T**	**W**	**Th**	**F**	**S**
			1	2	3	
4	5	6	7	8	9	10
11	12	13	14 ★	15	16	17
18	19	20	21	22	23	24
25	26	27	28	29	30	

June 14 is Flag Day. It celebrates the birthday of the American flag. Some cities have parades for Flag Day. Many Americans display the flag at their homes.

Flag Rules

DO display the flag higher than other flags.

DO shine a light on the flag at night.

DO fold the flag into a small triangle.

DON'T let the flag touch the ground.

DON'T draw on the flag or damage it.

DON'T fly the flag upside down.

Think and Solve

Study the infographic. Answer the questions.

1. What do the stripes stand for on the American flag?

    A. the 13 colonies

    B. the Fourth of July

    C. the 50 states

    D. the Civil War

2. A flag is two feet tall. About how long is it? _____ feet

3. Do not shine a light on the flag at night.

    True   **False**

4. Flag Day is celebrated in _____.

    A. January

    B. June

    C. July

    D. September

Color It

Color the American flag. Use the infographic to help you.

Do the Math

Draw 10 stars in each box.

_____   _____

How many stars in all? Count by tens. Write a number below each group of stars.

How many stars in all?

_____

How many states are in the United States of America?

_____

_____   _____

Write About It

In the star, write the name of your state. Write the name of your state's capital city.

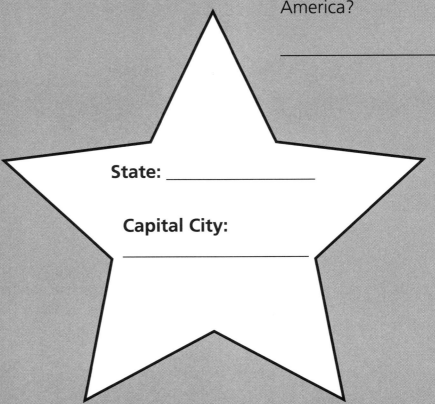

State: _____

Capital City:

_____

10 Reasons to Be a Farmer

1  You get to feed the world.

6  You can get dirty.

2 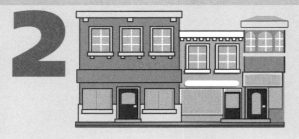 You get to work with your community.

7  You get to work with animals.

3  You can be proud of your harvest.

8  You can be around your family all day.

4 You get to work outside.

9 You get to care for the land.

5 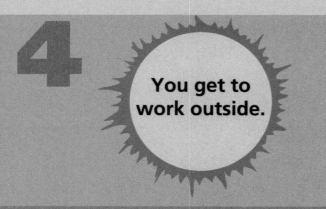 You get to ride on farm machines.

10  You will always have a job!

Study the infographic. Answer the questions.

1. Which reason is not one of the 10?

   A. You get to work outside.

   B. You can get messy.

   C. You can live in a farm house.

   D. You can be with your family.

2. List two things a farmer might grow.

_____

_____

3. What do you think *community* means?

   A. farm machines

   B. crops that a farmer grows

   C. people who live and work near you

   D. the buildings on a farm

4. Farmers get to work with animals.

True   **False**

Write About It

Would you like to be a farmer? Why or why not?

_____

_____

_____

_____

Read About It: Farmer Tucker's Busy Day

FARMER TUCKER GETS UP EARLY, at 5:00 in the morning. The sun is not even up yet. He eats breakfast. Then, Farmer Tucker goes to the chicken coop. It is 6:00 and time to gather eggs. The chickens cluck at him.

Farmer Tucker goes to the barn next. At 7:00, he milks the cows.

The sun is up in the sky now. Farmer Tucker gets on his tractor. He drives to the field at 9:00. Farmer Tucker will harvest crops. He works in the field for a long time.

At 5:00, Farmer Tucker drives back to the barn. He puts the tractor away. After dinner, it is 8:00. It is time to milk the cows again. The sun has set. It is dark outside.

Farmer Tucker is tired. He is glad it is time for bed!

Piece It Together

Cut apart the pictures that show parts of Farmer Tucker's day. Then, look at the clocks on page 45. Each clock shows a time when Farmer Tucker does something in the story on page 42. Glue or tape each picture next to the clock that shows when it happened.

		5:00	
		6:00	
		7:00	
		9:00	
		5:00	
		8:00	

Foods From American Indians

Many foods you eat today were first grown by American Indians.

Used in the past for...

Used today for...

Used in the past for...	Food	Used today for...
fried corn cakes	corn (maize)	biodiesel to run cars
making soup thicker	peanuts	soap and shampoo
baby food	wild rice	a burn remedy
treating sunburn	potatoes	stain remover
a hot drink	cocoa	moisturizer
flavored water	cranberries	an antibiotic
water containers	squash	soup
protein	beans	protein
an energy drink	maple tree sap	maple syrup
soup or sauce	avocado	skin creams

The Americas are divided into three areas. The map shows where each food was first grown. Match the colors in the chart on page 46 to the map.

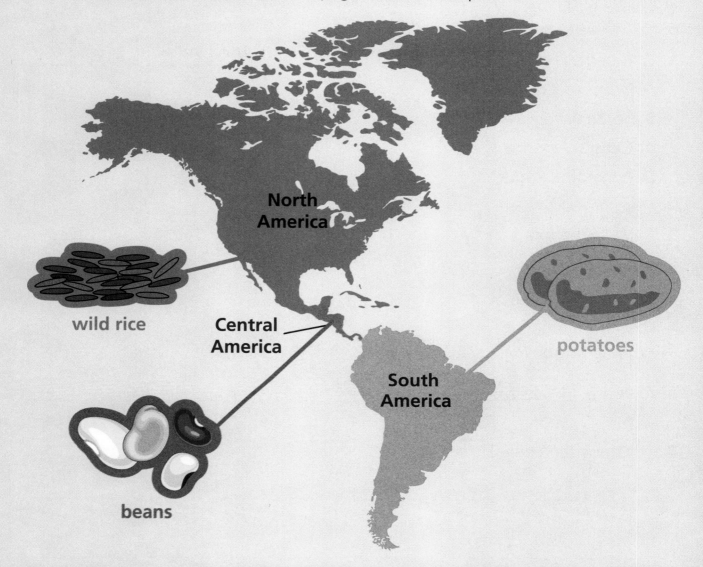

North America

wild rice

Central America

South America

beans

potatoes

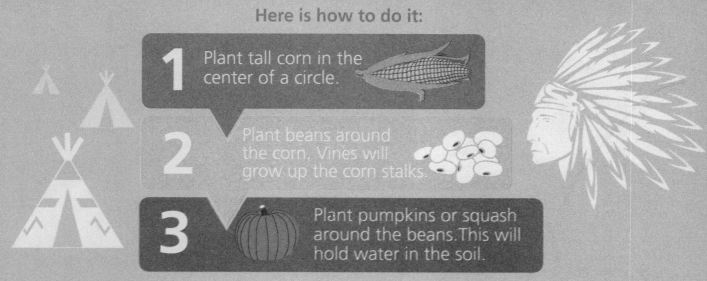

American Indians used a way of planting called the "Three Sisters."

Here is how to do it:

1 Plant tall corn in the center of a circle.

2 Plant beans around the corn. Vines will grow up the corn stalks.

3 Plant pumpkins or squash around the beans. This will hold water in the soil.

Think and Solve

Study the infographic. Answer the questions.

1. Cranberries were first grown in _____ .

   A. North America

   B. South America

   C. Central America

   D. none of the above

2. Most of the foods shown in the infographic were first grown in _____ .

   A. North America

   B. South America

   C. Central America

   D. none of the above

3. American Indians used peanuts in _____ .

4. What are the Three Sisters?

   _____

   _____

   _____

5. What did American Indians use for sunburn?

   A. potatoes

   B. wild rice

   C. chocolate

   D. avocado

Identify It

Look at the meals. Circle the foods that were first grown by American Indians.

Make a Plan

Plan a meal with foods from American Indians. Fill in each part of the menu.

Lunch Menu

Soup or salad

_____

Main dish

_____

Vegetable

_____

Fruit

_____

Dessert

_____

It All Makes Sense

You use your five senses every day to understand the world around you.

Sight

We see with our **eyes**.

Did you know your eyes are like video cameras?

Your brain records everything it sees. This helps you remember what everything looks like. Sight is the most used sense!

Hearing

We hear with our **ears**.

Did you know you have wax in your ears?

Earwax helps protect the ear by keeping it clear of dirt and dust. Earwax comes out all by itself!

Smell

We smell with our **nose**.

Did you ever notice that when you have a cold, you cannot smell anything?

That is because your nose is stuffy. It cannot get signals from your brain to tell what you are smelling!

Did you know?

Animals have senses, too. Dogs and sharks have a sharp sense of smell. Cats can see very well in dim light. Butterflies have taste organs on their feet, so they can taste anything they land on!

Touch

We feel with our **skin**.

Did you ever wonder why a stuffed animal feels so soft?

Nerve endings in your skin tell your brain how things feel when you touch them. It is the only sense you cannot turn off!

Taste

We taste with our **tongue**.

Did you ever taste something you did not like?

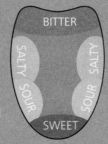

BITTER

SALTY SOUR SOUR SALTY

SWEET

Taste buds are found on your tongue. Most people have about 10,000 taste buds on their tongue!

Make Idea Webs

What do you sense? Look at the picture in the center of each web. Then, write a word on each arm of the web that describes the item using the sense.

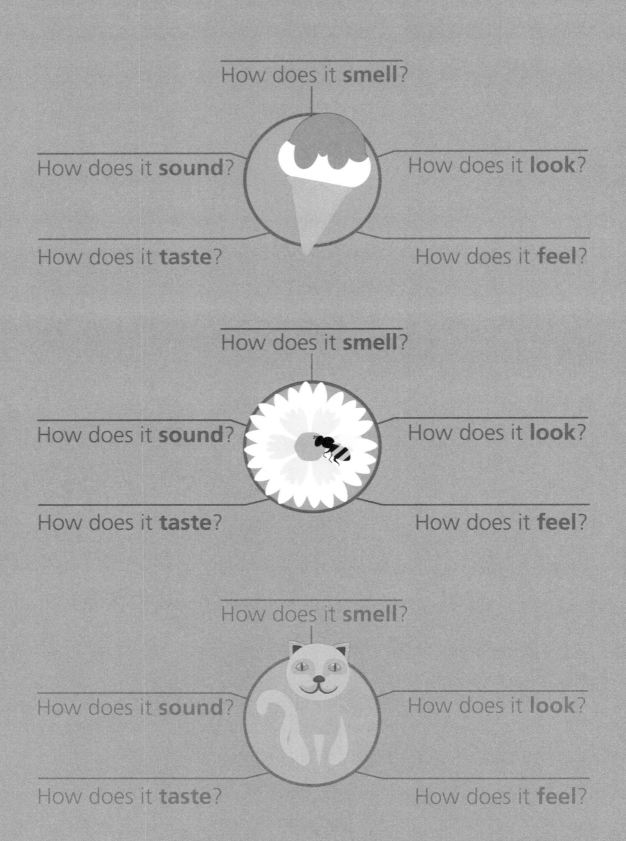

The Visual Guide to Kindergarten

Draw a picture in the center of the web. Then, write a word to describe what you drew using each sense.

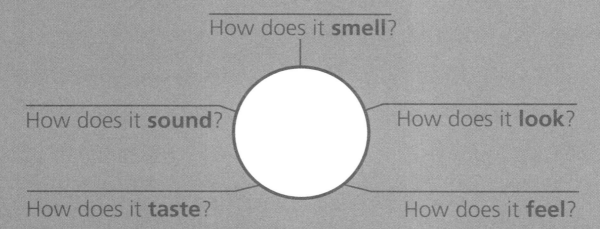

How does it **smell**?

How does it **sound**?

How does it **look**?

How does it **taste**?

How does it **feel**?

Guess It

Play a game with a friend. Think of an item. Write it on a line in the chart. Give clues that describe the item using each of the five senses. How many clues does your friend need to guess the item? Switch sides and have your friend give you clues about an item. Use the chart to keep track as you play.

Item

Going, Going, Gone

Kangaroo (35 mph)

Zebra (40 mph)

Elephant (25 mph)

Lion (50 mph)

Cottontail Rabbit (18 mph)

30   40

20   50

10   60

0   70

mph
(miles per hour)

Antelope (60 mph)

Squirrel (12 mph)

Spider (1 mph)

The average human runs 8 mph!
Athletes can run up to 40 mph!

Cheetah (70 mph)

The fastest bird (falcon)
flies over 200 mph!

Do the Math

Solve the problems. Use the infographic to help you.

1. How much faster is a lion than a zebra?

    A. 10 mph   **C.** 30 mph

    B. 20 mph   **D.** 40 mph

2. An elephant can run faster than _____ miles per hour.

    A. 20   **C.** 40

    B. 30   **D.** 50

3. How much faster is a cheetah than a lion? Choose the number sentence that will give the answer.

    A. 50 – 70   **C.** 70 – 50

    B. 70 + 50   **D.** 50 + 70

Try It Yourself

How fast are you? Find a one-mile path or trail at a nearby park or school. Then, ask an adult to time you as you run, walk, or bike for one mile.

How long did it take you to go one mile? _____ minutes

Now, find out how many miles you could go in one hour.

There are 60 minutes in one hour. Use the number of minutes you wrote above. Count by that number until you are near 60.

_____ _____ _____ _____ _____ _____

How many times did you need to count? Write the number to complete the sentence.

I went about _____ miles per hour.

All About Pumpkins

Pumpkins are ready to harvest in autumn. They are fun to carve. They are good to eat. What do you like to do with pumpkins?

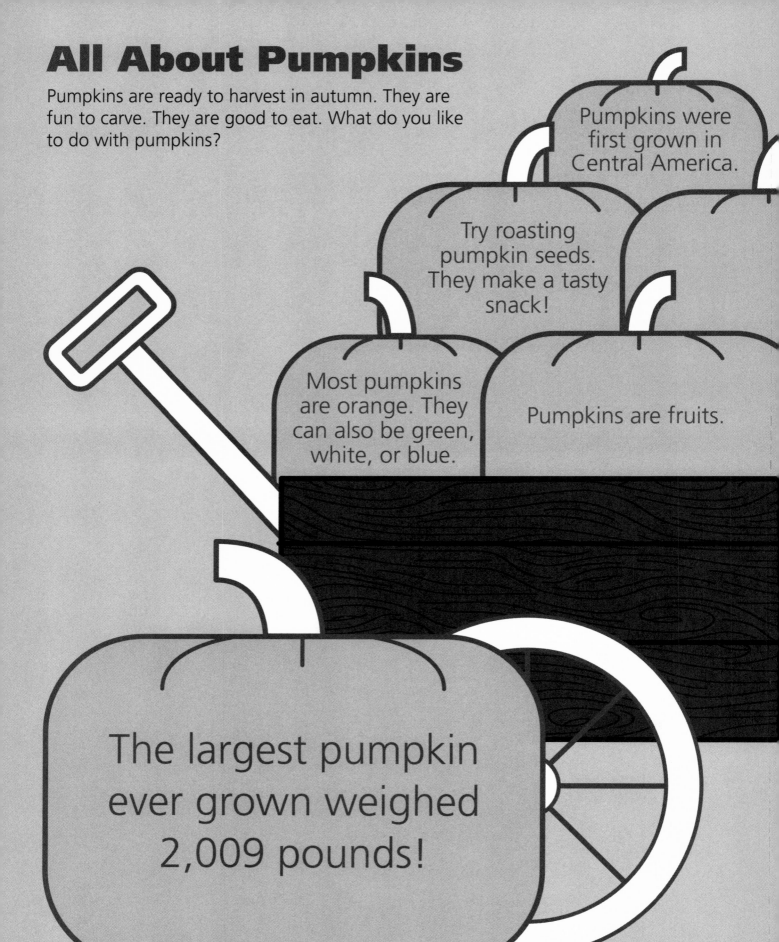

Pumpkins were first grown in Central America.

Try roasting pumpkin seeds. They make a tasty snack!

Most pumpkins are orange. They can also be green, white, or blue.

Pumpkins are fruits.

The largest pumpkin ever grown weighed 2,009 pounds!

More pumpkins are grown in Illinois than in any other state.

Pumpkins are used to make breads and soups. Many people eat pumpkin pie for Thanksgiving.

Pumpkins are a great source of vitamin A.

People carve pumpkins at Halloween. They are called *jack-o'-lanterns*. Some have spooky faces. Others have funny faces.

Think and Solve

Study the infographic. Answer the questions.

1. People carve jack-o-lanterns at _____ .

2. All pumpkins are orange.

True   **False**

3. What foods can you make with pumpkins? Name two.

_____   _____

Finish the Pattern

Draw the face on the jack-o-lantern that comes next in each pattern.

1.

2.

3.

Do the Math

Imagine you have $10 to spend at the pumpkin patch. Which pumpkins can you buy? Circle the combinations that add up to $10.

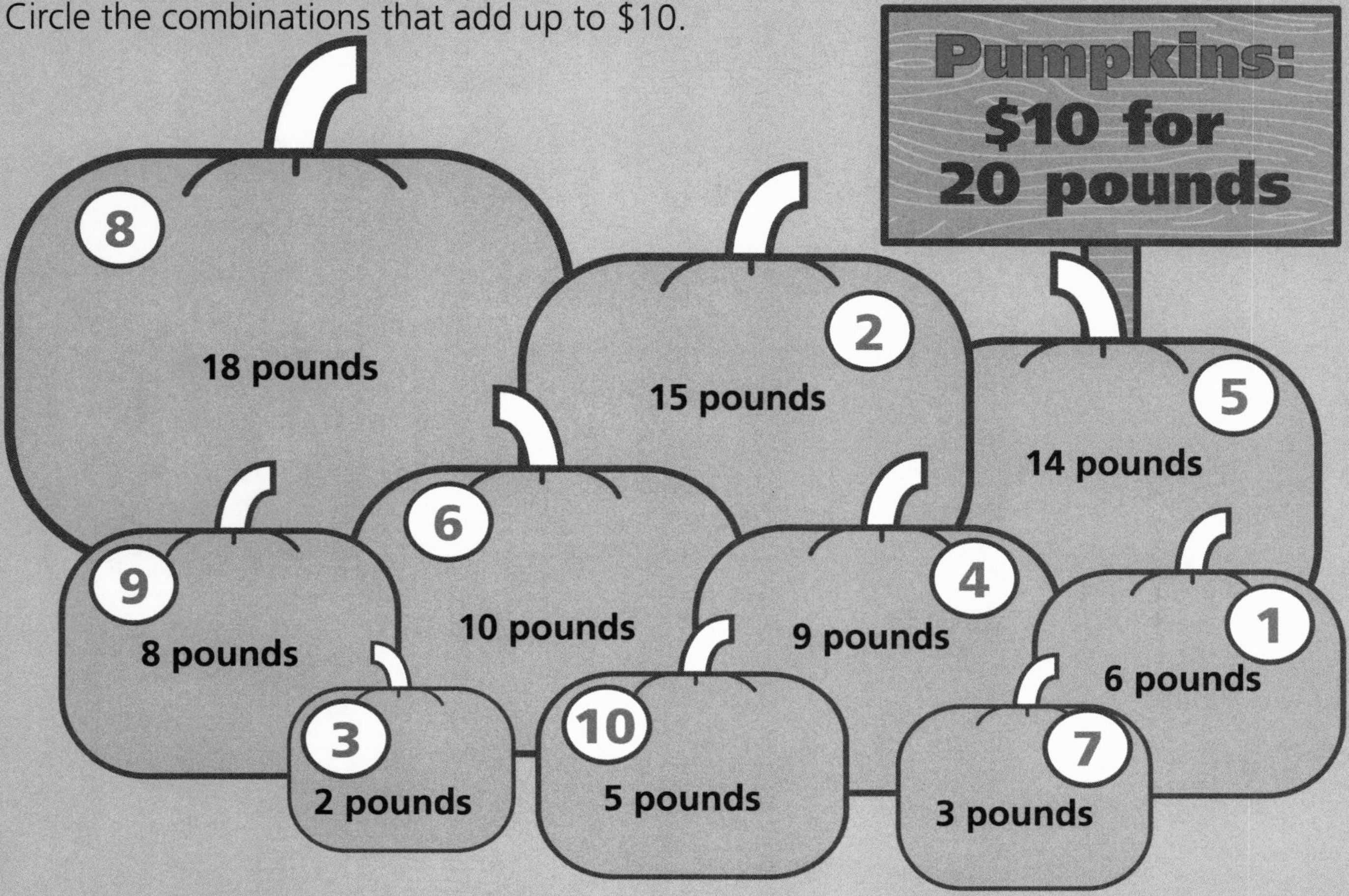

Pumpkins: $10 for 20 pounds

8 — 18 pounds
2 — 15 pounds
5 — 14 pounds
6 — 10 pounds
9 — 8 pounds
4 — 9 pounds
1 — 6 pounds
3 — 2 pounds
10 — 5 pounds
7 — 3 pounds

2 and 3 and 7

1 and 2

8 and 3

1 and 4 and 10

7 and 10

8 and 6

5 and 7

4 and 7 and 9

2 and 3 and 10

2 and 10

What to See in Washington, DC

Washington, DC, is the capital city of America. Special buildings in the city called *monuments* help us remember important people and events.

The Lincoln Memorial honors the 16th American president. Lincoln's famous words are carved in the walls.

The Thomas Jefferson Memorial stands beside a lake called the *Tidal Basin*. It honors the 3rd American president.

The Washington Monument has 897 steps! It honors the 1st American president.

Key:

has water

has many steps to climb

is made of stone

has statue of famous person

The Vietnam Veterans Memorial has the names of soldiers carved in black rock.

The World War II Memorial has two very tall arches. Each arch is 43 feet tall.

The Martin Luther King, Jr. Memorial honors the great black leader.

ABC has famous or important words

war monument

Think and Solve

Study the infographic. Answer the questions.

1. How many monuments are shown? _____

2. Which honors the 16th president?

   A. Lincoln Memorial

   B. Jefferson Memorial

   C. Washington Monument

   D. Martin Luther King, Jr. Memorial

3. All of the monuments are made of stone.

   True   False

4. What is the Tidal Basin? _____

Read About It: Chief Tecumseh

TECUMSEH WAS A LEADER OF THE SHAWNEE INDIANS. He was born in 1768. As a young man, he led battles against white settlers in Ohio and Indiana. He became Chief Tecumseh in 1800. Even though he fought the settlers, people in America and Britain admired him. He cared greatly for his people. In the War of 1812, he fought with the British against America. He died during battle. Chief Tecumseh is known today for his bravery and kindness.

Try It Yourself

Design a new monument for the city of Washington, DC. It will honor Chief Tecumseh. Will it have water? Will it be made of stone? Draw a picture of your monument. Then, finish the key. Color each symbol that describes your monument.

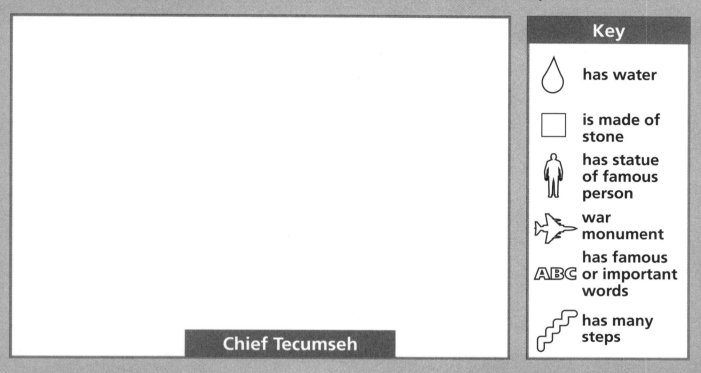

Chief Tecumseh

Key

○ **has water**

□ **is made of stone**

🚶 **has statue of famous person**

✈ **war monument**

ABC **has famous or important words**

🪜 **has many steps**

Schedule It

Imagine you are visiting Washington, DC. You want to see the monuments. Make a plan for your visit. Write the monuments you will see next to the times.

My Day in Washington, DC

9:00 A.M.	
10:00 A.M.	
11:00 A.M.	
12:00 P.M.	
1:00 P.M.	
2:00 P.M.	
3:00 P.M.	
4:00 P.M.	
5:00 P.M.	

The Mighty T. Rex

T. rex is known as the king of dinosaurs. How big was T. rex? How strong was T. rex? Scientists have learned a lot about the prehistoric king.

Height

T. rex	tree	house	you!
20 ft.	17 ft.	15 ft.	3½ ft.

Weight

18,000 lbs.	10,000 lbs.	1,100 lbs.	40 lbs.

Did you know a T. rex had...

very sharp teeth!

a brain shaped like a head of broccoli!

a jaw 6 times stronger than a crocodile!

Number of Teeth

about 50

about 75

28

20

Tail Length

about 20 ft.

4 ft.

3 ft.

1 ft.

Did you know a T. rex had...

eyes the size of half of a grapefruit!

feet that were 3 feet (or 1 yard) long!

arms too short to reach its mouth!

Think and Solve

Study the infographic. Answer the questions.

1. How many more feet long is an elephant's tail than a dog's tail?

_____

2. T. rex is known for having very long arms.

True   **False**

3. How tall was T. rex?

   A. 3 feet
   B. 20 feet
   C. 17 feet
   D. 15 feet

4. T. rex was about _____ feet taller than a tree.

Describe It

Color each footprint that has an adjective that describes T. rex.

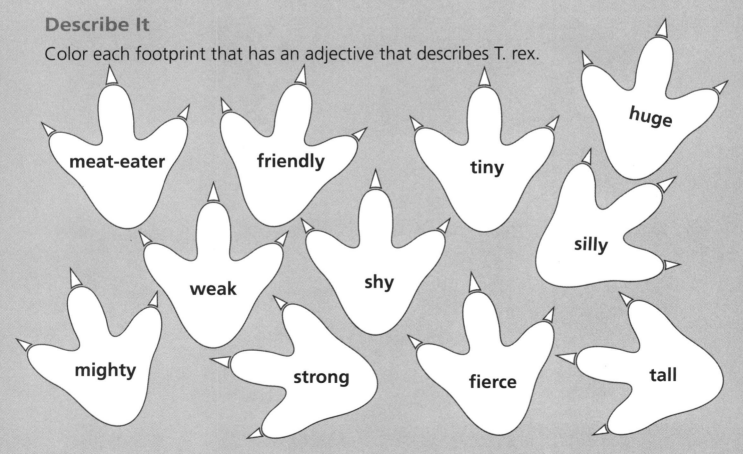

meat-eater   friendly   tiny   huge

weak   shy   silly

mighty   strong   fierce   tall

Piece It Together

Cut out the pieces along the dotted lines. Glue or tape them to page 69 to form a diagram of T. rex.

T. Rex

Tail
T. rex used its tail to balance its huge head.

Body
What color was T. rex? We don't know for sure. No skin has been found yet.

Legs
T. rex had very strong back legs. They helped it move quickly.

Arms
No one knows for sure why T. rex's arms were so short.

Head
T. rex had a strong jaw. It could eat about 500 pounds of meat in one bite.

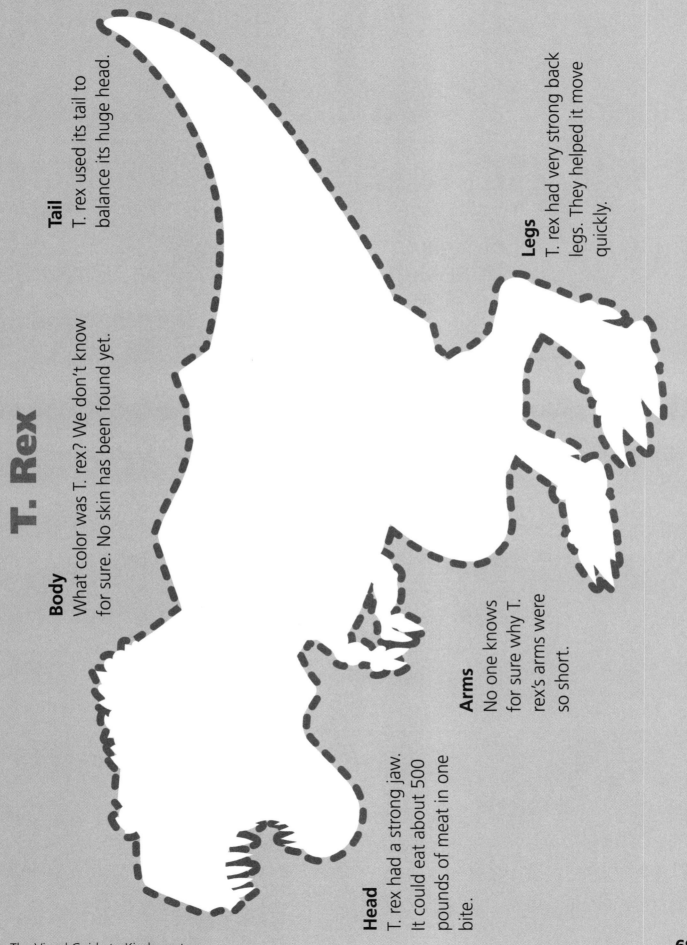

From Cow to Cone

How is ice cream made?

1 At a dairy farm, farmers milk the cows.

2 Fatty cream is skimmed from the top of the milk.

5 The mix is heated to kill harmful bacteria. This is called *pasteurizing*.

6 The ice cream mix is cooled quickly. It is whipped to add air and make it creamy.

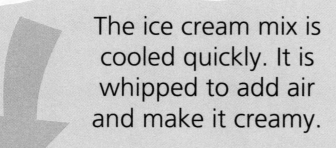

7 Then, chips, nuts, fruits, and other flavorings are added.

8 The ice cream is put into packages and frozen.

3

The cream and milk are delivered to the factory.

4

The milk and cream are mixed with sugar, eggs, and other ingredients.

10

9

The ice cream is delivered to stores and restaurants.

It is ready for you to eat.

YUM!

Think and Solve

Study the infographic. Answer the questions.

1. Which happens first? Circle the answer.

The mix is heated.   **The mix is whipped with air.**

2. Why is the mix heated?

    A. to make it soft

    B. to make it creamy

    C. to make it safe to eat

    D. to make it taste like chocolate

3. The nuts, fruits, or chips are added during Step _____ .

4. The ice cream is frozen before it is put in a package.

True   **False**

Make a Process Chart

Look at the pictures. Which can you do? Circle a picture that shows something you do well.

Make a Sandwich

Make the Bed

Make a Block Tower

Plant a Flower

Get Dressed

Set the Table

Now, tell how to do the thing you circled on the last page. Write the thing on the line. Draw or write each step in a box. The arrows show the order of the steps. You may not use all the boxes.

How to _____

What's Out There?

Far above Earth is space. What is found in space?

About 1 million Earths could fit inside the Sun!

Sun
The Sun is a huge, hot star. It keeps Earth warm. It helps plants grow. It gives Earth its light during the day.

Shooting Stars
A shooting star is really not a star at all. It is a small piece of rock or dust that moves so fast that it heats up and glows.

Satellites

More than 1,000 satellites orbit Earth! Satellites can show people where they are on Earth's surface. Satellites also tell us what the weather will be.

Earth
Earth is one of eight planets in our solar system. It is the only planet that people, plants, and animals live on.

Stars

Stars are giant balls of gas. Stars are usually between 1 and 10 billion years old. They can come in many colors such as red, blue, and orange.

Moon

The Moon does not have any wind, air, or rain. There are no living things on the Moon. The Moon gets really hot in the day and really cold at night.

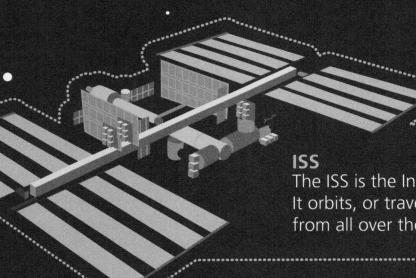

ISS

The ISS is the International Space Station. It orbits, or travels around, Earth. Scientists from all over the world work there.

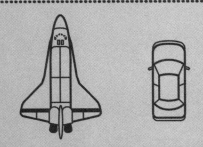

If you could drive to the Moon, it would take 153 days! A spaceship can make it there in about 2 days.

Think and Solve

Study the infographic. Answer the questions.

1. Our Sun is a star.

    True   **False**

2. What is another name for the International Space Station?

_____

3. What is a star?

    A. a giant rock

    B. a giant planet

    C. a giant ball of gas

    D. a giant ball of glowing dust

Match It

Draw a line from the pictures to their descriptions.

Shooting star

only planet with life

Sun

not really a star

Moon

keeps Earth warm

hot in the day, cold at night

Earth

Piece It Together

Cut apart the pictures of things that orbit (go around) Earth and the Sun. On page 79, glue or tape each picture in the correct column.

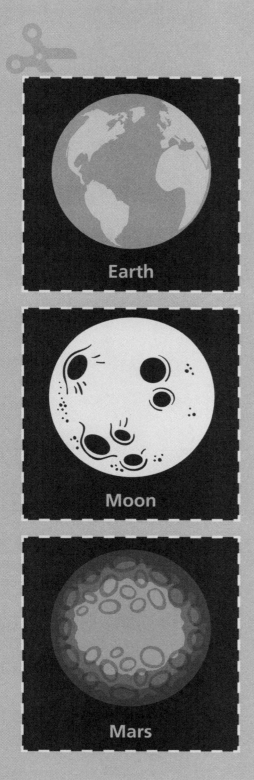

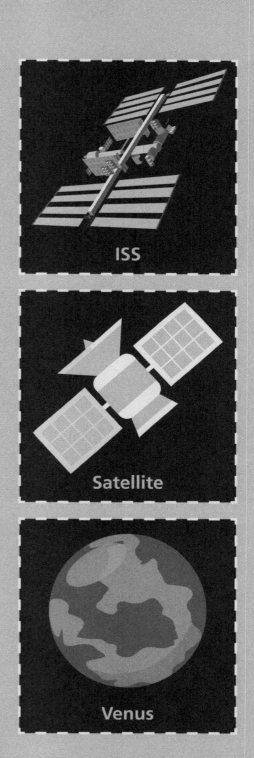

What Does It Orbit?

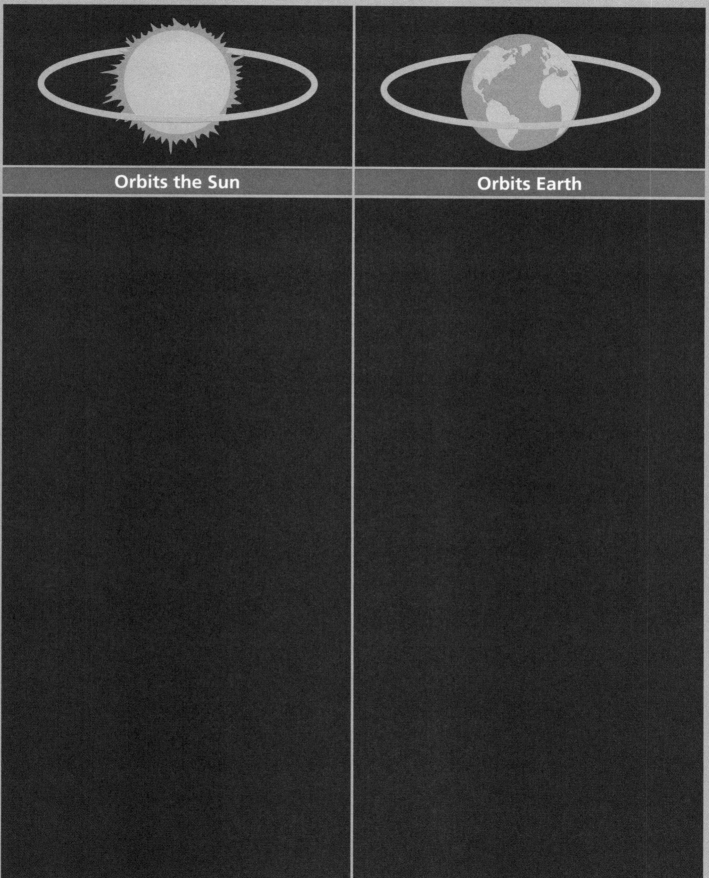

Orbits the Sun

Orbits Earth

Country Life and City Life

Some people love city life. Others love living in the country.
If you could choose, where would you live?

People who live in the country can grow their own food.

You can see tractors, trucks, and bikes in the country.

You can hear roosters crowing and crickets chirping
in the country.

You see many bright stars shining in the country night sky.

Is your home closer to a city or closer to the country?

People who live in the city can buy their food at the market.

You can see subways, taxis, and bikes in the city.

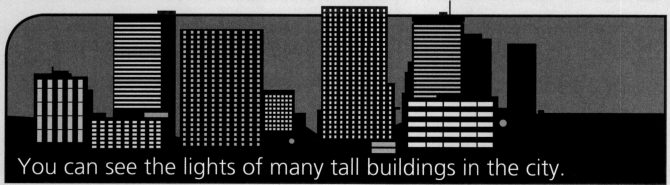

You can hear the sounds of busy traffic in the city.

You can see the lights of many tall buildings in the city.

Think and Solve

Study the infographic. Answer the questions.

1. If you have neighbors close by, you probably live in the

_____ .

2. The country is usually a quiet place.

True   **False**

3. Name three things that you might see in the city.

_____   _____   _____

4. Would you rather live in the city or in the country? Why?

_____

_____

_____

Classify It

Read each group of words. If it describes the city, write *CI*. If it describes the country, write *CO*. If it describes both, write *B*.

_____ lots of space	_____ a busy, noisy place	_____ big buildings
_____ grow own food	_____ starry nights	_____ people work there
_____ people live there	_____ houses and schools	
_____ farm animals	_____ subways, taxis, buses	

Compare and Contrast

Look at the list on page 82. Write the words that describe city life in the *City* circle. Write the words that describe country life in the *Country* circle. Write words that describe both in the middle.

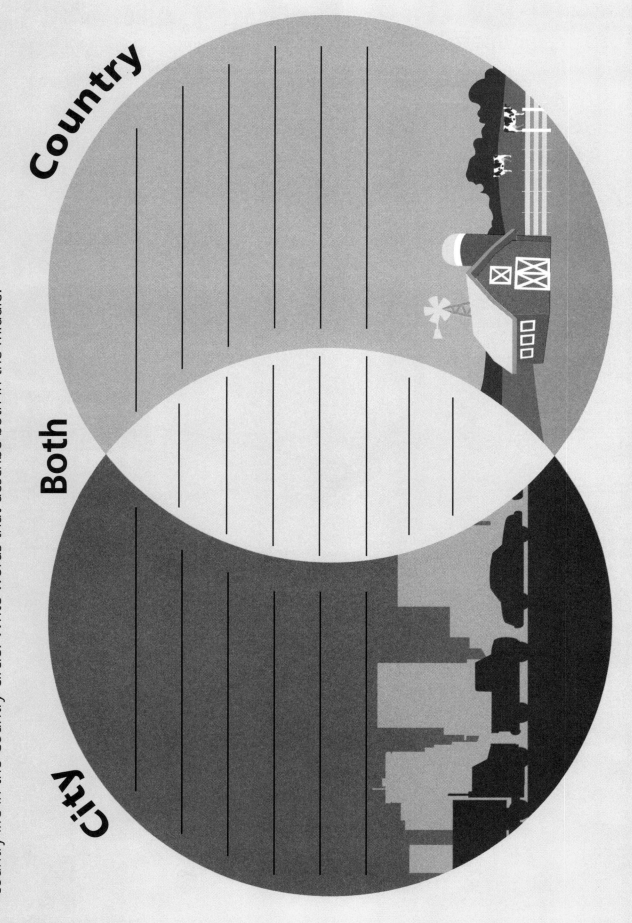

Country

Both

City

Special Days Around the World

Holidays are celebrated by people around the globe.

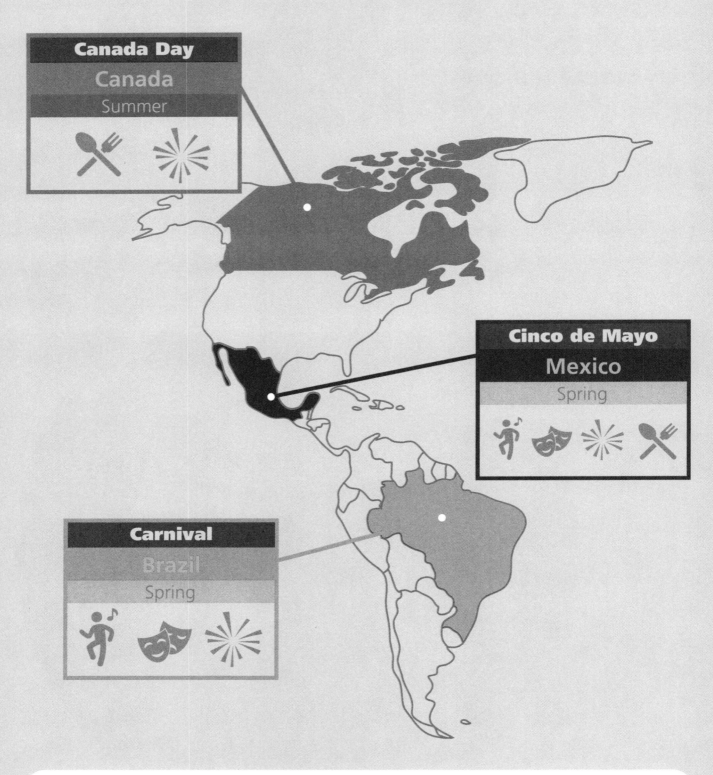

Canada Day
Canada
Summer

Cinco de Mayo
Mexico
Spring

Carnival
Brazil
Spring

Key:

 = dancing and music

 = lights

 = special foods

 = costumes

 = parades and festivals

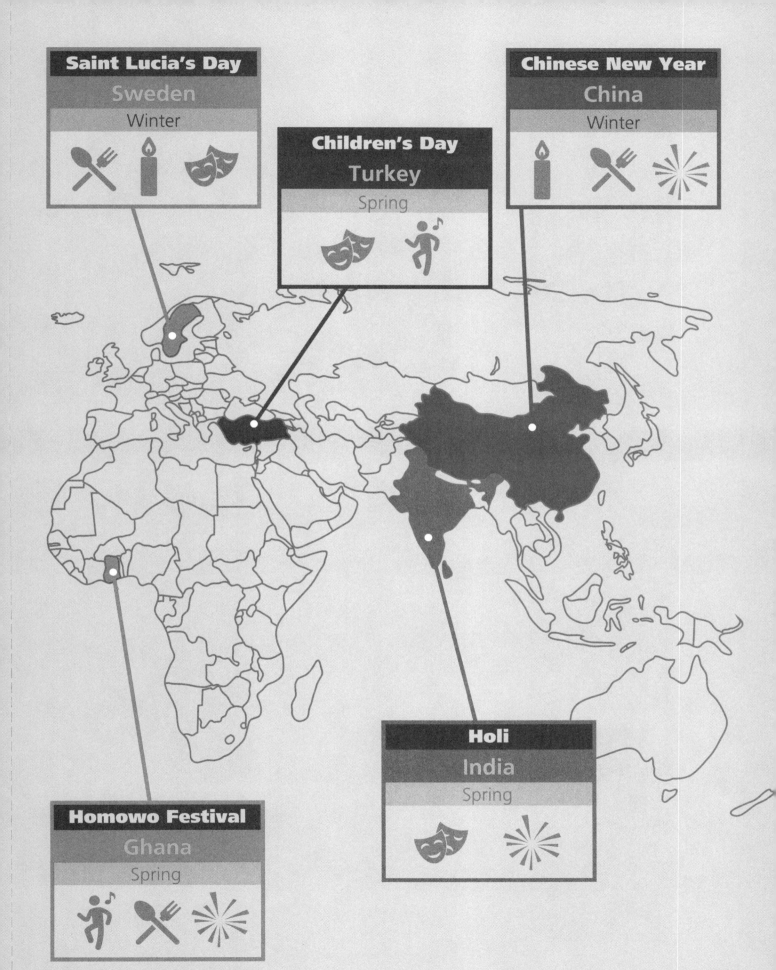

Saint Lucia's Day
Sweden
Winter

Children's Day
Turkey
Spring

Chinese New Year
China
Winter

Homowo Festival
Ghana
Spring

Holi
India
Spring

Label It

Write the names of the holidays on the continents where they are celebrated.

Children's Day	Chinese New Year
Cinco de Mayo	Homowo Festival
Carnival	Holi
Canada Day	Saint Lucia's Day

(Canada)

North America

(Mexico)

South America

(Brazil)

(Sweden)

Europe

(Turkey)

Asia

(China)

Africa

(Ghana)

(India)

Australia

Make a Chart

Make a check mark in each column that shows how your family celebrates the holiday. Then, add three holidays of your own. Make check marks for them, too.

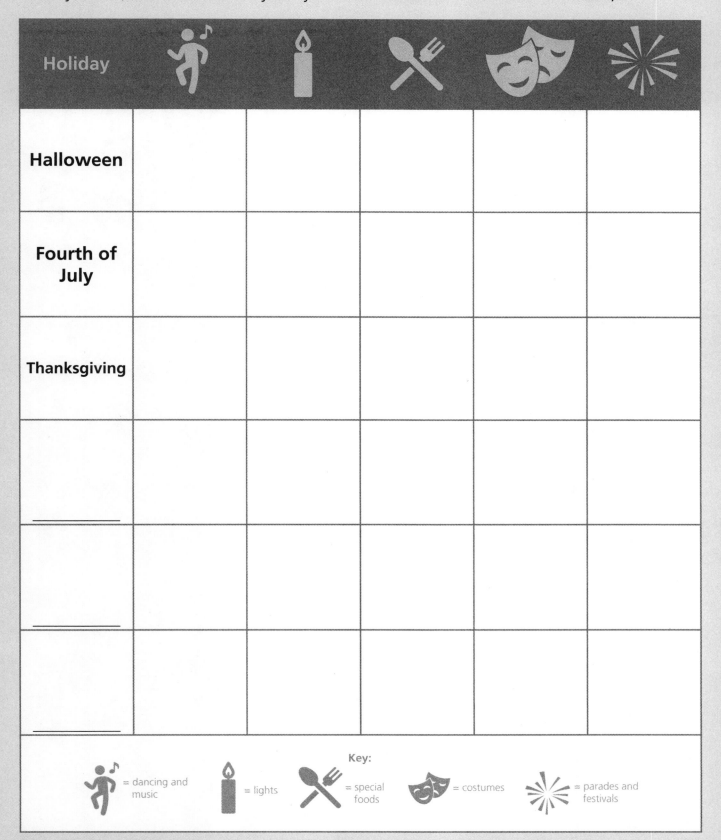

Holiday	🎵	🕯️	🍴	🎭	✳️
Halloween					
Fourth of July					
Thanksgiving					
_____					
_____					
_____					

Key:

= dancing and music = lights = special foods = costumes = parades and festivals

Pretty Patterns

A pattern is a repeated design. You can see patterns everywhere.

Animals

Tiger

Butterfly

Snake

Plants

Sunflower

Cactus

Leaves

Buildings

Windows

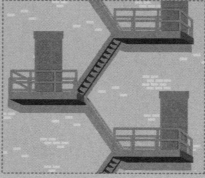
Stairs

Floors

Animal Homes

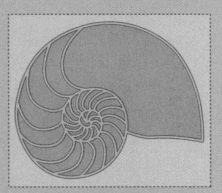

Shell

Honeycomb

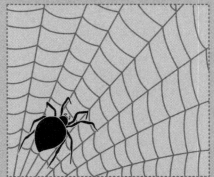

Spider Web

Fabrics

Plaid

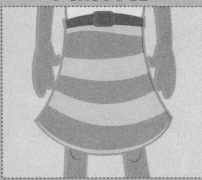

Stripes

Polka Dots

Nature

Clouds

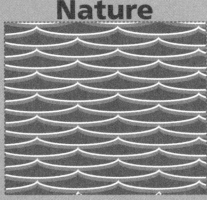

Water

Mountains

Classify It

Look at each picture. If it shows something living, write *L* on the line. If it shows something nonliving, write *N* on the line.

Show It

Finish coloring the picture. Complete the pattern.

Finish the Pattern

Look at each pattern. Write or draw what comes next.

Color It

Color the kittens and the basket. Each kitten should have a different pattern.

More Than One

Some brothers and sisters have the exact same birthday.

Brothers or sisters who are born on the same day are called TWINS.

IDENTICAL twins look just alike. But, they still have different fingerprints.

FRATERNAL twins look different.

The Visual Guide to Kindergarten

 **3** brothers or sisters who share a birthday are called TRIPLETS.

 **4** brothers or sisters who share a birthday are called QUADRUPLETS.

 **5** brothers or sisters who share a birthday are called QUINTUPLETS.

Animals can be multiples, too!

Solve the problems. Use the infographic to help you.

1. How many sisters or brothers are in two sets of twins?

   _____

2. One set of twins, one set of triplets, and one set of quadruplets are going to the park. How many kids are going to the park?

   _____

3. There are enough seats at the table for 10 kids. How many sets of quintuplets can sit there?

   _____

Match It

Match each group of brothers and sisters with the correct word.

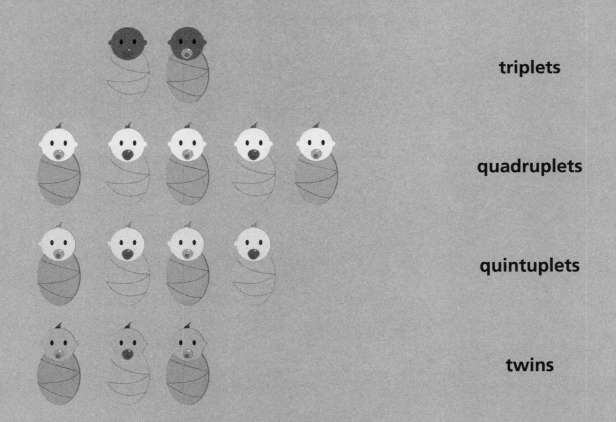

triplets

quadruplets

quintuplets

twins

Cut out the animal pictures. Glue or tape them to the chart on page 97.

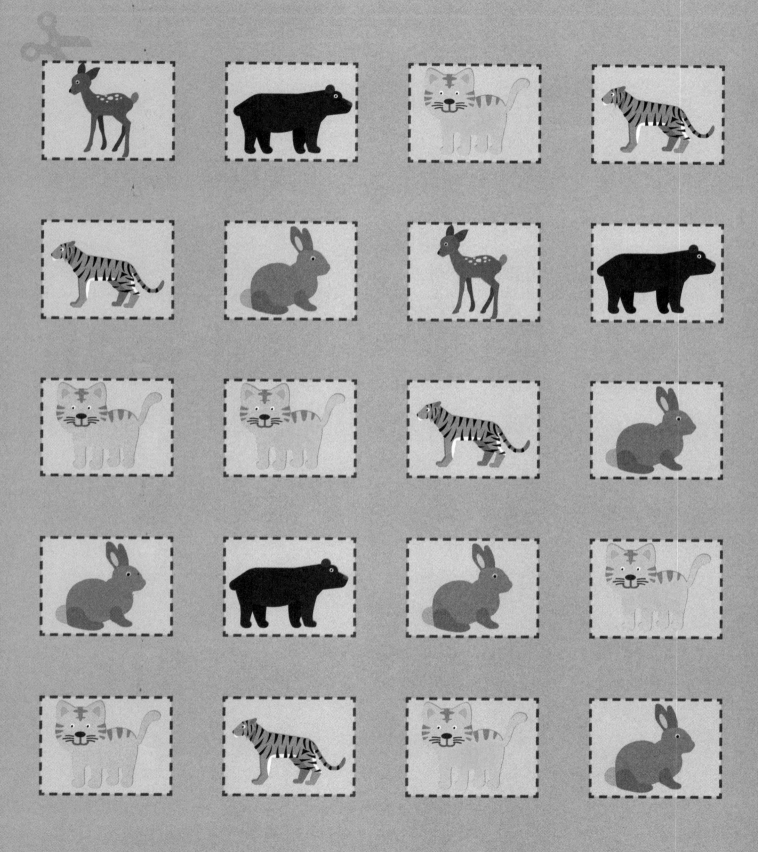

Twins	Triplets	Quadruplets	Quintuplets	Sextuplets

Neat Seeds

Seeds need sun, water, and soil to grow.

Seeds

A seed is the part of a plant that can grow into a new plant.

A Seed Can Travel

by wind

by animal

by water

by you!

Neat Fact!
The largest seed in the world is the seed of a palm tree. It can weigh up to 44 pounds (20 kg). That's about as much as you weigh!

Think and Solve

Study the infographic. Answer the questions.

1. A seed is the part of a plant that can grow into a new _____ .

2. The largest seed in the world comes from _____.

    A. an oak tree

    B. an orange tree

    C. a palm tree

    D. an apple tree

3. Have you ever planted a seed? What kind was it?

_____

_____

Sequence It

In each story, write 1, 2, and 3 to put the steps of the seed's journey in order.

_____ The seeds fly into the soil in Sam's yard.

_____ Seeds stick to Sam's pants when he plays at the park.

_____ At home, Sam brushes off his pants in the yard.

_____ The robin flies away. Waste comes out of its body.

_____ A robin sits on a bush. It eats blackberries.

_____ Seeds in the robin's waste drop to the ground.

Money Matters

Each US coin or paper bill has a different value.

Penny
Value: **1¢**

President:
Abraham Lincoln

The year tells when the coin was made.

Nickel
Value: **5¢**

President:
Thomas Jefferson

Dime
Value: **10¢**

President:
Franklin D. Roosevelt

Quarter
Value: **25¢**

President:
George Washington

One-Dollar Bill

Value: **100¢ or $1**

President:
George Washington

The torch and branches stand for liberty (freedom), peace, and strength.

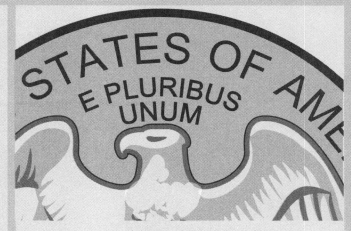

These Latin words mean "Out of many, one."

The dollar bill is made of cotton and linen. It has tiny strings of silk running through it.

The print on the front of a dollar bill is black.

The print on the back is green. Dollar bills are sometimes called *greenbacks*.

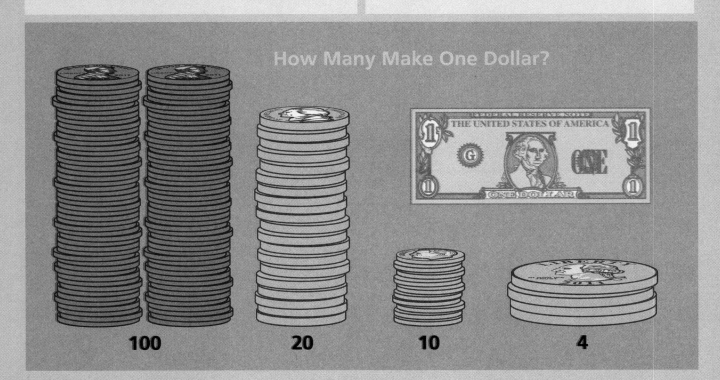

How Many Make One Dollar?

100   20   10   4

Think and Solve

Study the infographic. Answer the questions.

1. It takes 20 dimes to make one dollar.

    True   **False**

2. Which president is on the front of the quarter?

    A. Washington   **C.** Jefferson

    B. Lincoln   **D.** Roosevelt

3. If you have six pennies, then you have _____ cents.

Do the Math

Add the value of the coins. Write the total on the line.

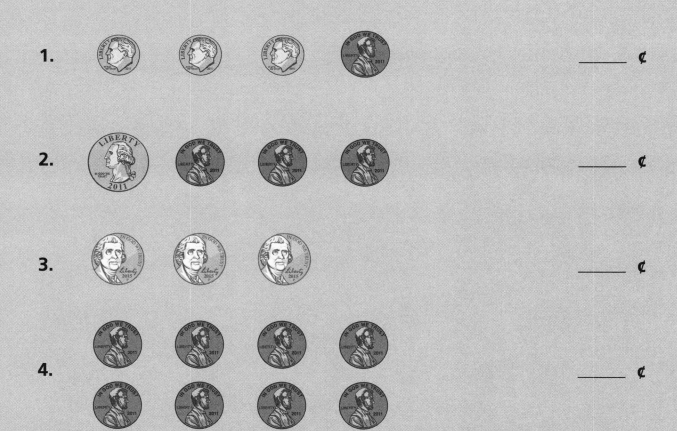

1. _____ ¢

2. _____ ¢

3. _____ ¢

4. _____ ¢

Collect all the coins you can find. If you have a coin jar or a piggy bank at home, ask an adult if you can look at the coins inside. Then, find the date on each coin. Make a check mark for each type of coin you find for each year.

Year	Penny	Nickel	Dime	Quarter
2006				
2007				
2008				
2009				
2010				
2011				
2012				
2013				
2014				
2015				

A Way to Go

There are many ways to travel. People travel on land, in the water, and in the air.

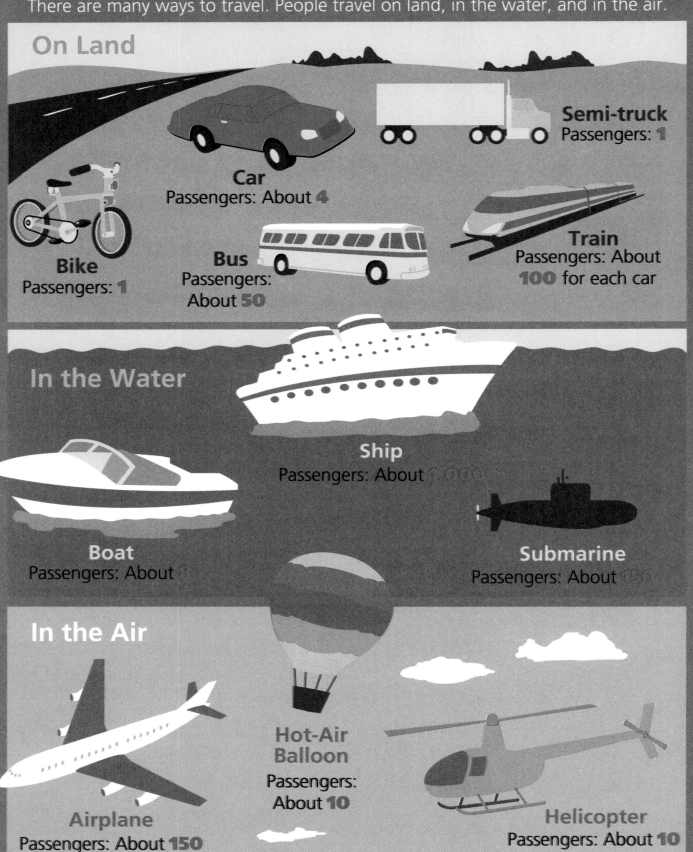

On Land

Car
Passengers: About 4

Semi-truck
Passengers: 1

Bike
Passengers: 1

Bus
Passengers: About 50

Train
Passengers: About 100 for each car

In the Water

Ship
Passengers: About 1,000

Boat
Passengers: About 8

Submarine
Passengers: About 150

In the Air

Airplane
Passengers: About 150

Hot-Air Balloon
Passengers: About 10

Helicopter
Passengers: About 10

Do the Math

Solve the problems. Use the infographic to help you.

1. 12 people go on a trip. How many cars do they need?

_____

2. How many more people can go in a boat than in a car?

_____

3. 16 people are on an island. A helicopter will move them all to another island. How many trips does the helicopter need to make?

_____

4. 3 people get in the basket of a hot-air balloon. How many more people can the hot-air balloon carry?

_____

Make a Bar Graph

How do you travel? Keep track for five days. Each time you go somewhere, color a block to show how you went.

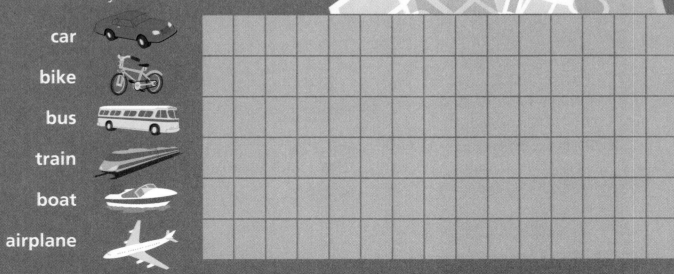

car

bike

bus

train

boat

airplane

Carved in Stone

The faces of four American presidents are carved into Mount Rushmore in South Dakota. Millions of people visit each year.

George Washington was the **1st** American president. He stands for the **birth** of our country.

Thomas Jefferson was the **3rd** American president. He made the country **grow** by adding new land.

It took almost **20** years to complete Mount Rushmore!

❚ = 1 year

Washington had all his teeth pulled. He wore false teeth made of ivory.

Jefferson loved to read and write. He owned more then 6,000 books. He wrote more than 19,000 letters in his lifetime!

Roosevelt loved hiking, camping, and the outdoors. He once climbed a 15,000-foot mountain!

When he was young, **Lincoln** was a great wrestler. He lost only one time out of 300 matches!

Abraham Lincoln was the **16th** American president. He helped keep the country **together**.

Theodore Roosevelt was the **26th** American president. He helped **build** our country.

Think and Solve

Study the infographic. Answer the questions.

1. Mt. Rushmore is in South Carolina.

   True   **False**

2. _____ was the first American president.

3. Which president kept the country together?

   A. Washington

   B. Jefferson

   C. Roosevelt

   D. Lincoln

Match It

Draw a line to match each president to a fact.

He had false teeth.

He added land to our country.

He loved being outdoors.

He was a great wrestler.

Label It

Write a president's last name under each face on Mt. Rushmore.

_____

_____

_____

_____

Imagine It

Imagine you are the president of the United States. What will you do to help your country? Write your ideas.

_____

_____

_____

_____

_____

The Lovely Ladybug

A little red dot lands on your arm. The friendly little
critter means you no harm. It's a ladybug!

Ladybugs are about as big as a pencil eraser.

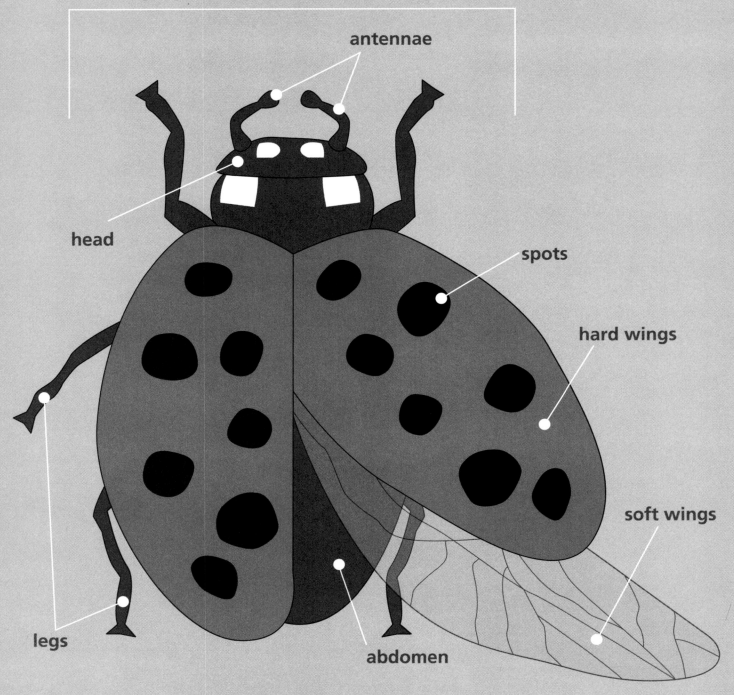

antennae

head

spots

hard wings

soft wings

legs

abdomen

Did you know. . .
she beats her wings
85 times per second?

Did you know. . .
she uses her front
legs to wash her face?

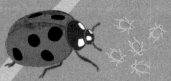

Did you know. . .
she is lucky for farmers
because she eats bugs
that are bad for
the plants?

Did you know. . .
her spots get lighter
as she gets older?

Did you know. . .
she is not just red and
black? She can come in
many colors like pink,
yellow, white, and
orange, too.

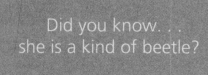

Did you know. . .
she is a kind of beetle?

Did you know. . .
she hibernates? Ladybugs sleep
in huge groups to stay warm.

Think and Solve

Study the infographic. Answer the questions.

1. A ladybug has two kinds of wings: _____ and _____.

2. A ladybug is a kind of beetle.

   True   **False**

3. All ladybugs are red.

   True   **False**

Do the Math

How many spots in all?

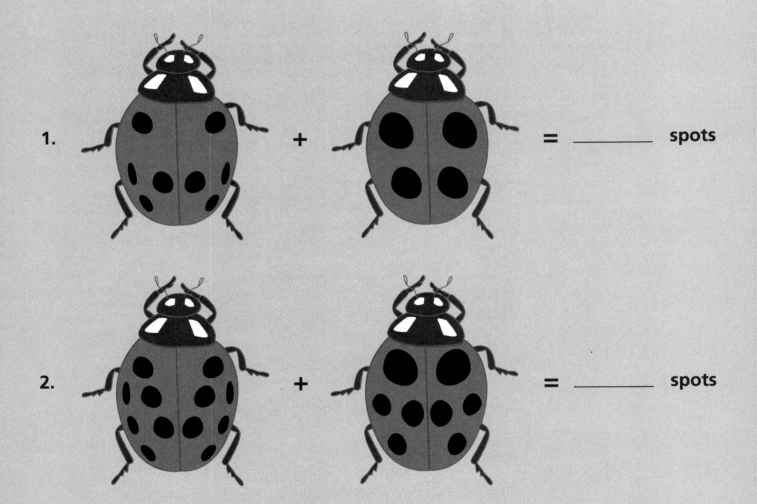

1. _____ + _____ = _____ spots

2. _____ + _____ = _____ spots

Label It

Label the parts of the ladybug. Then, color the insect.

head	leg	soft wing	hard wing
antenna	abdomen	spot	

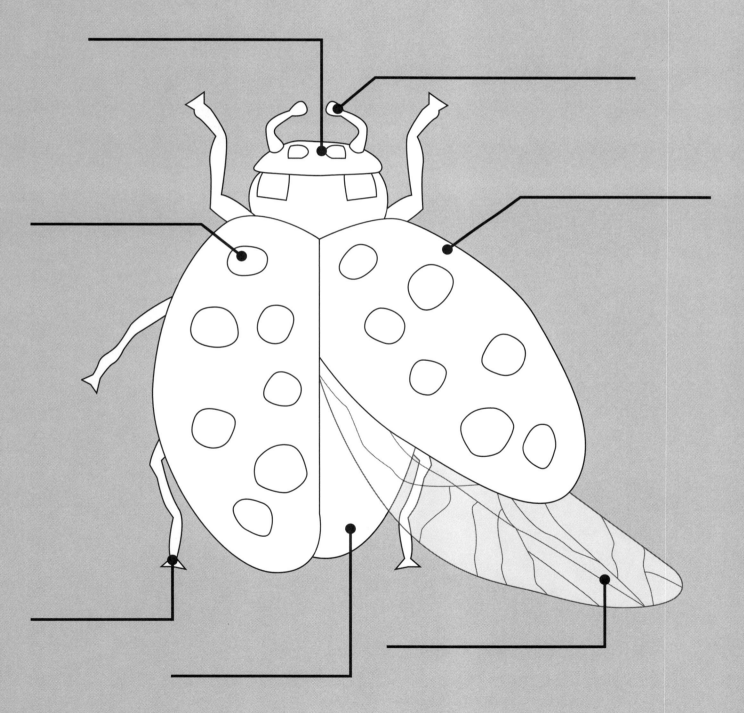

Edison's Amazing Inventions

Many people think that Thomas Edison was the greatest inventor in history!

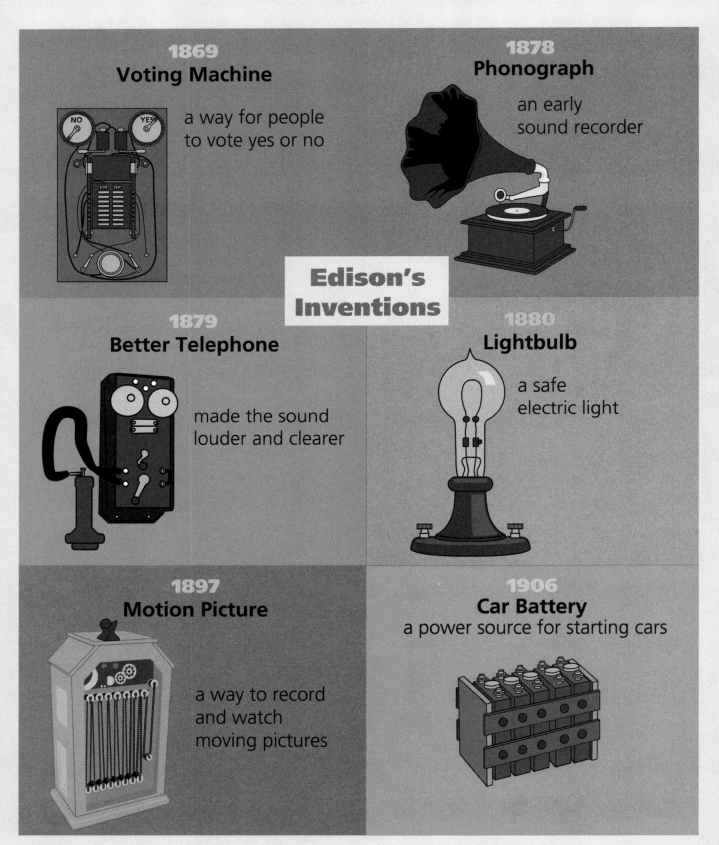

1869
Voting Machine

a way for people to vote yes or no

1878
Phonograph

an early sound recorder

Edison's Inventions

1879
Better Telephone

made the sound louder and clearer

1880
Lightbulb

a safe electric light

1897
Motion Picture

a way to record and watch moving pictures

1906
Car Battery
a power source for starting cars

Did You Know That Thomas Edison . . .

 was partly deaf?

 set up a lab in his basement at age 10?

 published his own newspaper at age 12?

 created over 1,000 inventions?

 saved a child from being run over by a train?

 was the first person to show a movie?

 slept only three or four hours each day?

 was famous around the world?

Think and Solve

Study the infographic. Answer the questions.

1. Thomas Edison was almost blind.

True   **False**

2. How old was Edison when he set up a basement lab?

_____

3. Edison had _____1,000 inventions.

  A. less than   **B.** more than

Match It

Draw a line from the invention to the year it was made.

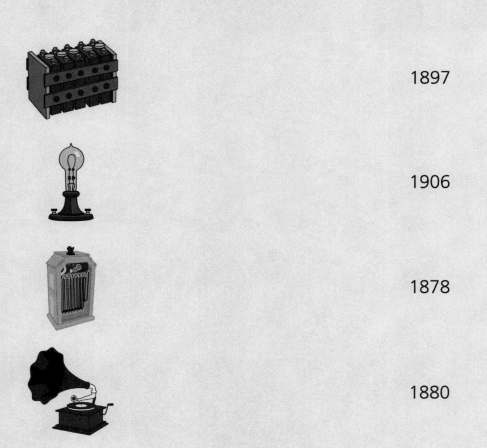

1897

1906

1878

1880

Make an Idea Web

Choose five adjectives that describe Thomas Edison. Write them in the web.

| lazy | smart | famous | sad | loud |
| hardworking | tired | great | safe | brave |

Imagine It

Design a new invention. Draw it in the box. Then, write about it on the lines.

Oceans Alive

Many animals live in the ocean. The bigger animals need the smaller ones for food. A *food chain* shows how animals survive in the ocean.

plankton

krill

small fish

mackerel

tuna

shark

The ocean food chain starts with plankton. Plankton are tiny creatures that make their own food from sunlight. Krill eat plankton. Small fish eat the krill. Bigger fish eat the smaller fish.

The sun provides energy.

plankton

krill

small fish

squid

seal

killer whale

Seals and killer whales are ocean mammals. They are part of the ocean food chain, too. Killer whales eat seals. Seals eat squid. Squid eat small fish. Small fish eat krill, which feed on plankton.

Think and Solve

Study the infographic. Answer the questions.

1. A killer whale is not a fish.

True   **False**

2. The ocean food chain begins with _____.

    A. squid

    B. plankton

    C. krill

    D. sharks

3. How many different sea creatures are shown in the infographic?

_____

4. Plankton make their own food.

True   **False**

Read About It:
Finding Food in the Forest

PLANTS AND ANIMALS IN THE FOREST ARE PART OF A FOOD CHAIN, too. Plants need sunlight. They use the light to make their own food. Insects and small animals eat the plants. Frogs and rats eat the insects. A snake might eat a frog or a rat. Then, a bigger animal such as a hawk or a fox might eat the snake. In the forest, just like in the ocean, bigger animals need smaller animals in order to survive.

Piece It Together

What do animals eat in the forest? Review the passage on page 120. Cut apart the pictures of plants and animals that make up a forest food chain. Glue or tape them in the correct places on page 123.

snake

plant

grasshopper

hawk

frog

A Forest Food Chain

The Liberty Bell

The Liberty Bell is a huge metal bell that can be seen today in Philadelphia, Pennsylvania. In the early days of America, the bell was rung for important events.

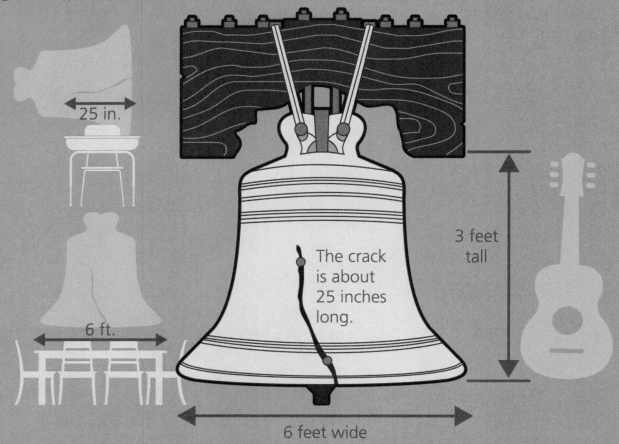

25 in.

6 ft.

The crack is about 25 inches long.

3 feet tall

6 feet wide

1752
The Liberty Bell was made.
It cracked during a test ringing.

1753
The Liberty Bell was fixed.
It was hung inside the
steeple of a building.

1776
The Liberty Bell was rung to celebrate the
Declaration of Independence.

1777
The Liberty Bell was hidden during the
Revolutionary War.

1787
The Liberty Bell was
rung to celebrate the
US Constitution.

1750   1760   1770   1780   1790

The Liberty Bell can no longer ring, but it is still a symbol of freedom.

When did the bell ring?

 On the 4th of July

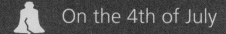 To call people together

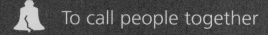 To announce a new president

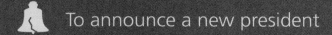 To remind people to vote

On George Washington's birthday

1835
The Liberty Bell cracked for the second time.

1852
The Liberty Bell was taken down from the steeple. It was put inside a building.

| 1810 | 1820 | 1830 | 1840 | 1850 | 1860 |

Think and Solve

Study the infographic. Answer the questions.

1. The Liberty Bell is about _____ feet wide.

2. The Liberty Bell cracked during a war.

   True   **False**

3. Circle which happened first.

   The Liberty Bell was rung to celebrate the Declaration of Independence.

   The Liberty Bell cracked for the second time.

4. When was the Liberty Bell hidden?

_____

Explore Your World

The Liberty Bell is three feet, or one yard, tall. Ask an adult to help you find a yardstick. Use it to measure things inside and outside. Draw two things you find that are about as tall as the Liberty Bell.

3 feet tall

Write About It

Liberty means "freedom." America has many symbols of freedom. Some of them are shown below. Circle your favorite.

Statue of Liberty

American Flag

Liberty Bell

Bald Eagle

Freedom is an important part of being an American. Tell how the symbol you circled shows freedom. Explain why freedom is important to you.

_____

_____

_____

_____

_____

_____

_____

Toys From Around the World

Children all over the globe love to play with toys.

Children in Africa make toy vehicles called *galimotos*. These toys are made from recycled trash such as old wire, bits of plastic, and ribbon.

Children in China play with colorful shapes called *tangrams*. Seven pieces, called *tans*, are used to create a picture. All seven pieces must be used. They must lay flat. They must touch but not overlap.

Children in the United Kingdom play tiddlywinks. This game is played with small discs called *winks* and a pot. Players try to shoot a disc into the pot by flicking it off of another disc, which sends it flying through the air.

Children in India play a table game called *carom*. Players flick discs with their fingers. They try to get them in the corner pockets.

Did you know?

Children have played with marbles for thousands of years. Marbles were found in Egyptian pyramids!

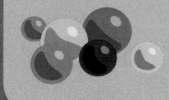
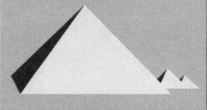

One of the oldest board games is called the *Royal Game of Ur*. It is more than 4,000 years old!

Children in Russia play with nesting dolls. Each wooden doll fits inside the next. All of the dolls fit inside the largest one.

Children in Mexico play with marionetas. Marionetas are puppets made of wood and fabric. They have strings that make them move.

Children in the Philippines play a game called *sungka*. It uses a wooden board. The board has bowls carved in it. Each player tries to collect the most shells (or pebbles) in the end bowls.

Children in the Netherlands enjoy a game called *sjoelbak*. It is played on a long board. The goal is to slide wooden circles into openings at the end of the board.

The teddy bear is named after American president Teddy Roosevelt.

Long ago in America, dolls were made of corn husks.

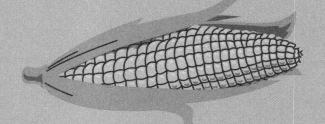

Think and Solve

Study the infographic. Answer the questions.

1. Where do children play with nesting dolls?

    A. China

    B. Russia

    C. India

    D. United Kingdom

2. Who is the teddy bear named after?

_____

3. Marbles have been around for thousands of years.

True   **False**

4. Which game or toy from around the world would you like to play with? Why?

_____

Sequence It

Write 1, 2, 3, 4, or 5 on each line to put the steps in order.

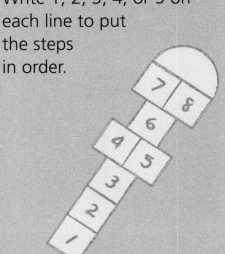

How to Play Hopscotch	
_____	Pass the beanbag or rock to the next player.
_____	Throw a small beanbag or rock to land on a square.
_____	Pick up the beanbag or rock on your way back.
_____	Hop through the squares. Skip the one where your beanbag or rock landed.
_____	Draw a hopscotch grid on the ground.

Try It Yourself

These items are often used in children's games. Circle three you would like to use in your own game.

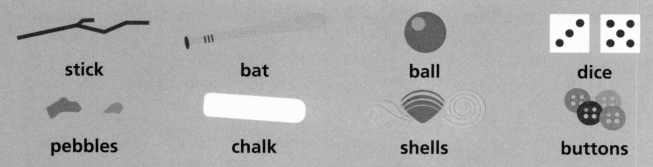

stick   bat   ball   dice

pebbles   chalk   shells   buttons

Tell how to play your game. In each space, draw and write to explain one part of the game.

Now, play your new game alone or with friends!

Happy Birthday!

How long do animals live?

A life span is the time between an animal's birth and its death.

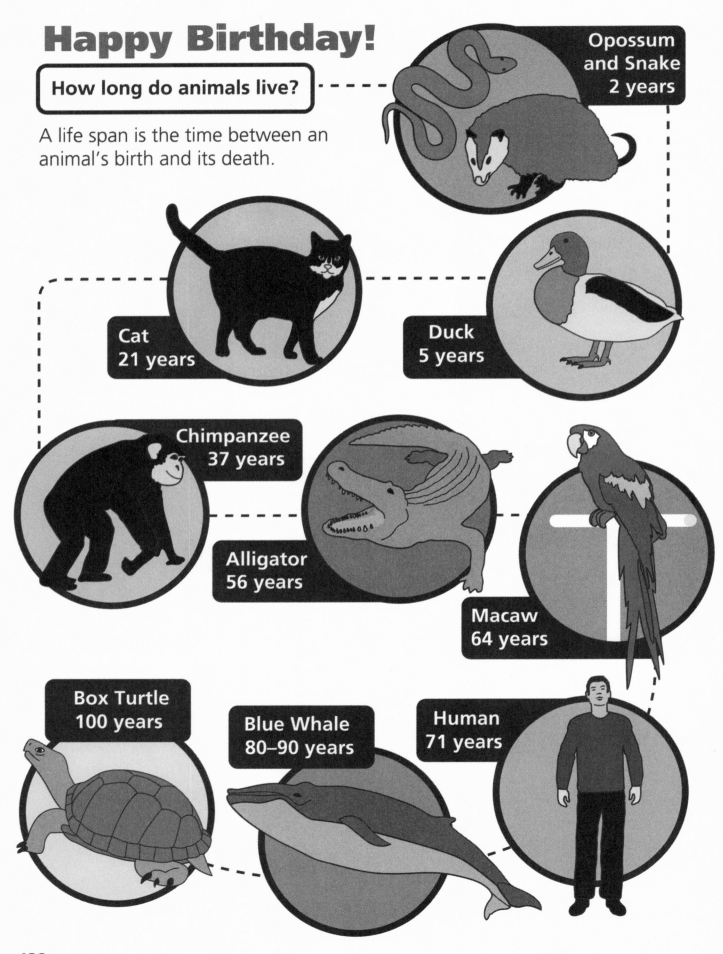

Opossum and Snake
2 years

Cat
21 years

Duck
5 years

Chimpanzee
37 years

Alligator
56 years

Macaw
64 years

Box Turtle
100 years

Blue Whale
80–90 years

Human
71 years

Think and Solve

Study the infographic. Answer the questions.

1. Which animal lives the longest?

    A. human

    B. box turtle

    C. macaw

    D. blue whale

2. An opossum and a snake have the same life span.

    True   **False**

3. How many reptiles are in the infographic? _____

Do the Math

Solve the problems. Use the infographic to help you.

1. A duck lives _____ years longer than a snake.

2. A dog lives for 14 years. How much longer does a cat live?

_____

3. A frog lives twice as long as a duck. How long does a frog live?

_____

4. A mouse in the wild lives half as long as an opossum. How long does a mouse live?

_____

Looking for Freedom

The Pilgrims crossed the ocean to find freedom.
They solved many problems along the way.

New World Bound!

Problem
Some people in England could not practice their own religion.

Solution
More than 100 Pilgrims sailed to the New World on the *Mayflower*.

Problem
There were 0 rules for people to follow in the New World.

Solution
41 male Pilgrims wrote and signed the *Mayflower Compact* on November 11, 1620.

Problem
There were 0 stores in the New World, so Pilgrims had to find their own food.

Solution
American Indians taught them to hunt, fish, and grow their own food.

MAYFLOWER

The Pilgrims had their first harvest in the fall of 1621. The Pilgrims wanted to thank the Wampanoag for their help. They invited the American Indians to share in a big feast. It was the first Thanksgiving.

Invitation

To: The Wampanoag

Come for: A Thanksgiving Feast

Thank you for: Helping us plant and harvest crops

Menu: Duck or turkey, corn, peas, shellfish, carrots, blueberries, cranberries, squash, and plums

A 3,000-Mile Journey

The *Mayflower* sailed from Plymouth, England, to the New World. The journey took 66 days.

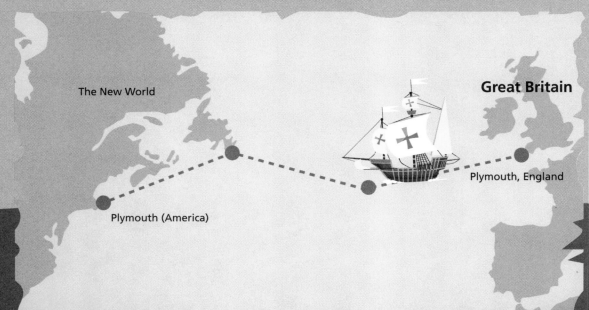

The New World

Great Britain

Plymouth, England

Plymouth (America)

Think and Solve

Study the infographic. Answer the questions.

1. What was the name of the Pilgrims' ship?

    A. the *New World*

    B. the *Mayflower*

    C. the *Plymouth*

    D. the *Wampanoag*

2. Before America became a country, it was called the *New World*.

    True   **False**

3. The American Indians invited the Pilgrims to a feast.

    True   **False**

4. The Pilgrims began their journey in _____.

    A. Plymouth, America

    B. the New World

    C. Plymouth, England

    D. Canada

5. Why did the Pilgrims go to the New World?

    A. to meet the American Indians

    B. to hunt and grow their own food

    C. to look for freedom

    D. to explore the world

Match It

Who said it? Read each sentence. Draw a line to the person who might say it.

I will show you how to hunt.

I am looking for freedom.

I come from far away.

Please come to our feast.

We will share our land.

I will show you how to grow plants.

Write About It

Imagine that a Thanksgiving feast will be at your home. Complete the invitation.

To: _____

Please come to our Thanksgiving feast!

Where: _____

When: _____

Menu: _____

_____

Know Your Snow!

Snowflakes form when water freezes in the air. Other frozen forms of water are ice, sleet, and hail.

Snow is made up of snowflakes and air.

- Snow is actually clear. It reflects light and can look white or blue.

- It is probably not a good idea to eat snow. Snow can contain animal waste, pollution, and dirt.

- You can make a snowman, ride a sled, and make snow angels in the snow.

Igloos are special houses made of blocks of hard-packed snow. The snow acts as an insulator to keep the people who live in igloos warm.

The tallest snow woman was built in Maine. She stood 122 feet (37.2 m) tall. Her name was Olympia. She wore a giant red hat and had blond hair made from rope. Her eyelashes were made from skis and her buttons were old truck tires.

Piece It Together

Cut out the snowman pieces. Glue or tape the snowman's body on page 141. Then, decorate it with the pieces you like.

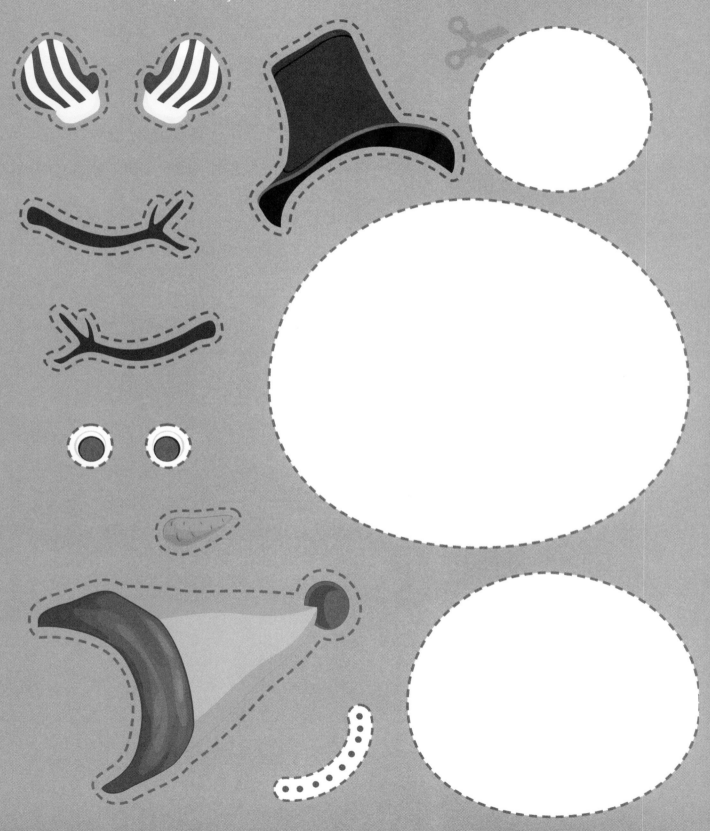

Build a Snowman

The Inuit People

The Inuit people are American Indians. They live in
the far north on the frozen tundra.

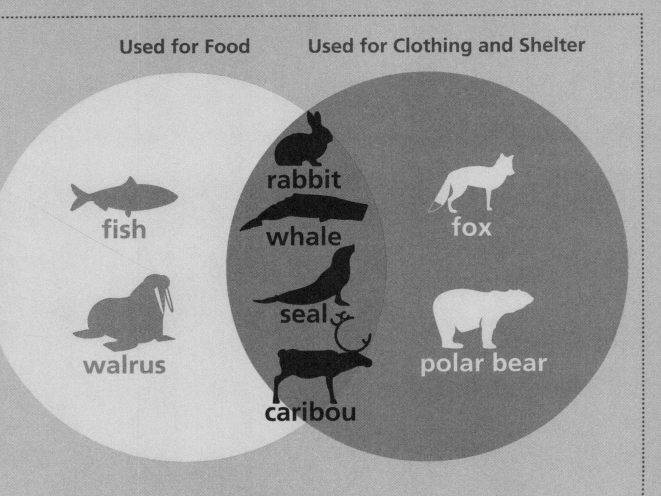

Used for Food   **Used for Clothing and Shelter**

fish

rabbit

whale

fox

walrus

seal

caribou

polar bear

The tundra is not good for farming. In the old days, the Inuit
lived by hunting. They used the animals of the Arctic for meat.
They used animal skins to make warm clothes. They even used
skins to make tents and cover canoes. Today, life in the Arctic
has changed a lot. Most things are modern. But in some ways,
the Inuit still try to keep the old ways alive.

This is a view of
the Arctic from the
top of the world,
looking down.

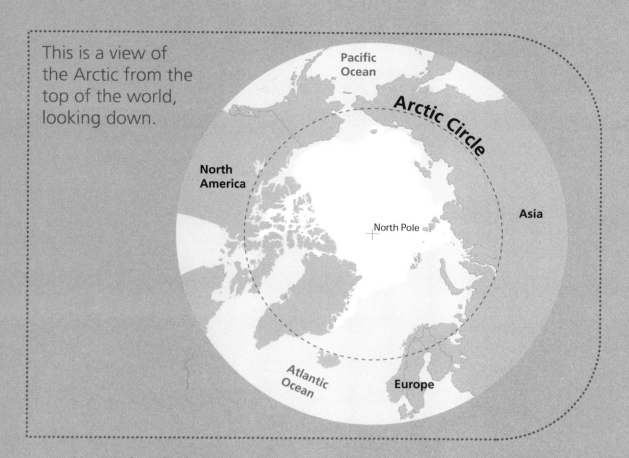

Pacific
Ocean

Arctic Circle

North
America

Asia

North Pole

Atlantic
Ocean

Europe

An Inuit Dictionary ◄

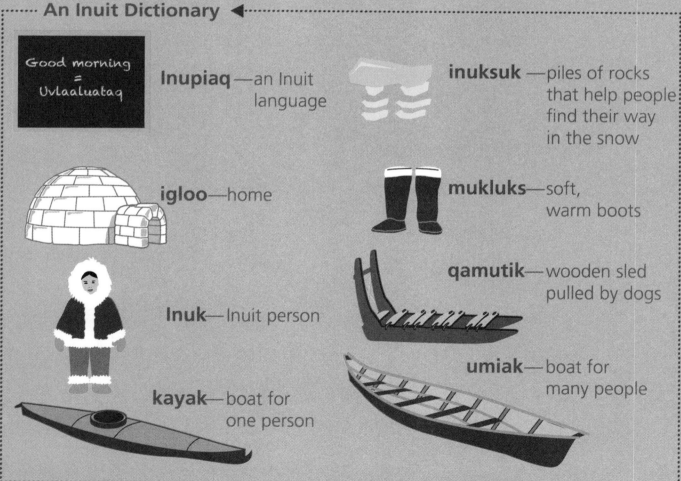

Good morning
=
Uvlaaluataq

Inupiaq—an Inuit
language

inuksuk—piles of rocks
that help people
find their way
in the snow

igloo—home

mukluks—soft,
warm boots

Inuk—Inuit person

qamutik—wooden sled
pulled by dogs

kayak—boat for
one person

umiak—boat for
many people

Think and Solve

Study the infographic. Answer the questions.

1. Name one way the Inuit used animal skins.

_____

2. An Inuk is not a member of the Inuit people.

True   **False**

3. Mukluks are worn on the _____.

4. Describe an igloo.

_____

Match It

Draw a line to match each picture to its meaning.

wooden sled pulled by dogs

boat for many people

boat for one person

home

Label It

Write the name of each Arctic animal. Use the words in the box. Circle the animals that the Inuit used for both food and clothing/shelter.

fox	**whale**	**seal**	**fish**
walrus	**caribou**	**polar bear**	**rabbit**

_____

_____

_____

_____

_____

_____

_____

_____

Crossing the Globe

Many animals and insects *migrate*, or move from one place to another. Some migrate because they need more food. Others migrate because of the weather.

Gray Whales

These giant sea animals migrate very far. They move farther than almost any other mammal. Gray whales travel from the ocean near Alaska to warmer water near Mexico. The trip takes two to three months. Scientists have seen that they swim faster in the warmer water.

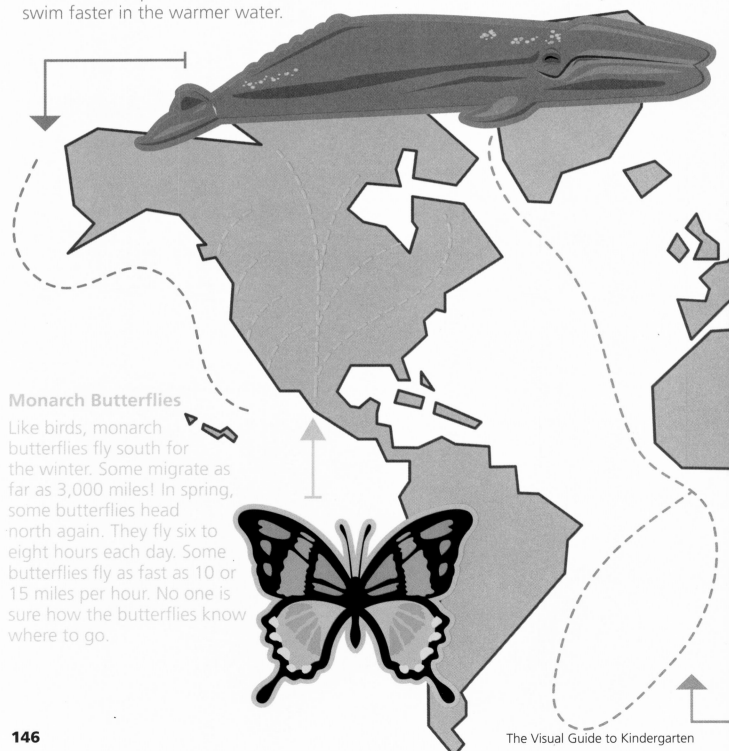

Monarch Butterflies

Like birds, monarch butterflies fly south for the winter. Some migrate as far as 3,000 miles! In spring, some butterflies head north again. They fly six to eight hours each day. Some butterflies fly as fast as 10 or 15 miles per hour. No one is sure how the butterflies know where to go.

Gnus

Gnus are also called *wildebeests*. More than one million of them are on the move in Africa. They migrate looking for grass to eat. The path they follow is shaped liked a giant circle. Many other animals travel with them, including zebras. Lions, crocodiles, and hyenas are a danger to gnus.

Arctic Terns

The Arctic tern flies all the way from the North Pole to the South Pole! Then, it flies all the way back again. It is the only bird that migrates so far. Terns often fly back to the same spot where they hatched.

Think and Solve

Study the infographic. Answer the questions.

1. How is a monarch butterfly like a bird?

    A. It has wings.   **C.** It migrates.

    B. It flies.   **D.** all of the above

2. A gray whale swims faster in warm water.

    True   **False**

3. Why do you think a lion is a danger to a gnu? _____

    _____

Match It

Draw a line from each animal to a fact about it.

   It migrates from the North Pole to the South Pole.

     It moves in a path shaped like a giant circle.

   No one is sure how it knows where to migrate.

   It migrates from Alaska to Mexico.

Use a Calendar

The calendar shows when each animal migrates. Use it to answer the questions.

= Gray Whales

= Monarch Butterflies

= Arctic Terns

= Gnus

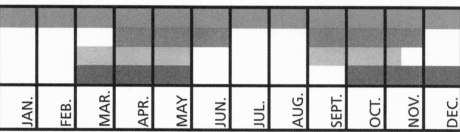

| | JAN. | FEB. | MAR. | APR. | MAY | JUN. | JUL. | AUG. | SEPT. | OCT. | NOV. | DEC. |

1. Which animal is on the move all year long?

_____

2. When are all four creatures migrating?

    A. March

    B. June

    C. October

    D. December

3. Arctic terns are migrating for _____ months of the year.

4. Monarch butterflies do not migrate during the winter.

    True   **False**

A Crop of Corn

Corn is the largest and most important crop grown on farms in America.

Hundreds of strands, called *silk*, grow from the top of each ear of corn.

A *tassel* grows at the top of the plant.

Each ear of corn has about 500 corn *kernels* in about 15 rows.

Leaves help the plant collect light from the sun.

Ears of corn are tightly wrapped in *husks*.

Each plant grows one to four *ears of corn*.

The tall plant grows on a *stalk*.

Roots reach deep into the soil to find food and water for the plant.

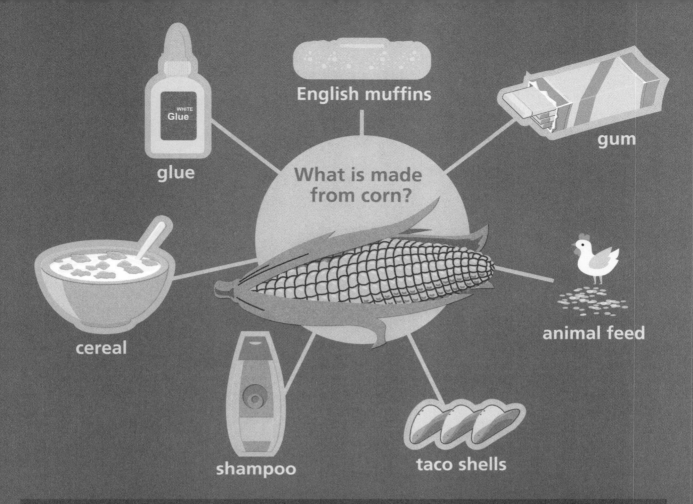

glue

English muffins

gum

What is made from corn?

cereal

animal feed

shampoo

taco shells

How are every 10 bushels of corn used in America?

To feed animals

To make gasoline

Sold to other countries

To feed people in America

Think and Solve

Study the infographic. Answer the questions.

1. You can use corn to _____.

    A. make gasoline

    B. feed animals

    C. feed people

    D. all of the above

2. Each ear of corn has about _____ rows of kernels.

3. Out of every 10 bushels of corn grown in America, how many are used to feed animals?

    _____

4. Name one food you eat that has corn in it.

    _____

5. Most of the corn grown in America is used to make gasoline.

    True   False

6. How many ears of corn can be grown on two corn plants?

    A. about 12

    B. about 10

    C. about 2

    D. about 6

Explore Your World

What crops grow near your home? Find out by looking for farmers' fields, by reading books or websites, or by asking adults. Try to visit farms near your home and look closely at the plants growing there. Then, draw a picture of three crops that grow in your city or state. Write the name of each one.

Log It

Keep track of the vegetables you eat each day for one week. Beside each day, make a check mark to show each vegetable you ate.

	Corn	Carrots	Lettuce	Peas	Green Beans	Potatoes	Broccoli	Peppers	Other
Sunday									
Monday									
Tuesday									
Wednesday									
Thursday									
Friday									
Saturday									

Professor Carver's Peanuts

George Washington Carver, born a slave, was a famous scientist and inventor who loved to help others.

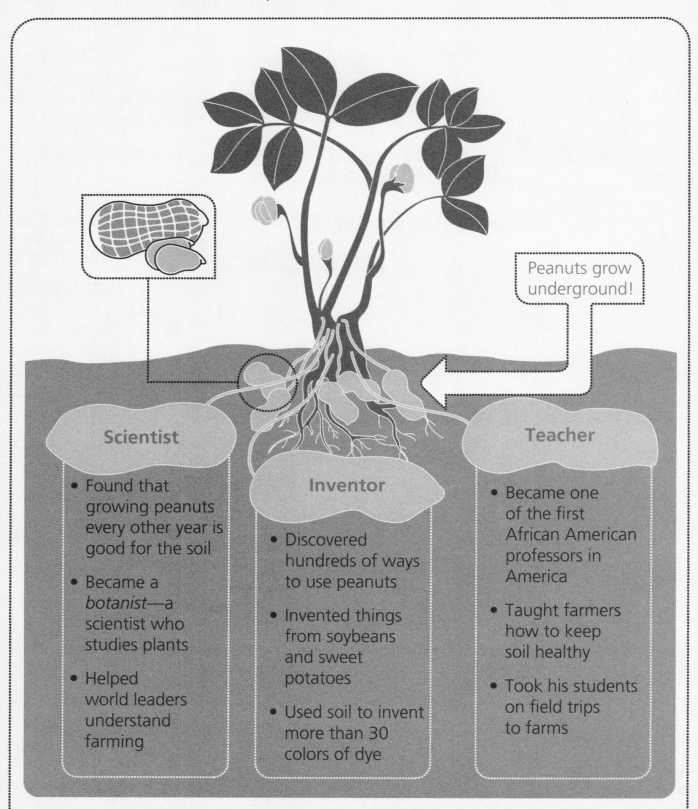

Peanuts grow underground!

Scientist

- Found that growing peanuts every other year is good for the soil
- Became a *botanist*—a scientist who studies plants
- Helped world leaders understand farming

Inventor

- Discovered hundreds of ways to use peanuts
- Invented things from soybeans and sweet potatoes
- Used soil to invent more than 30 colors of dye

Teacher

- Became one of the first African American professors in America
- Taught farmers how to keep soil healthy
- Took his students on field trips to farms

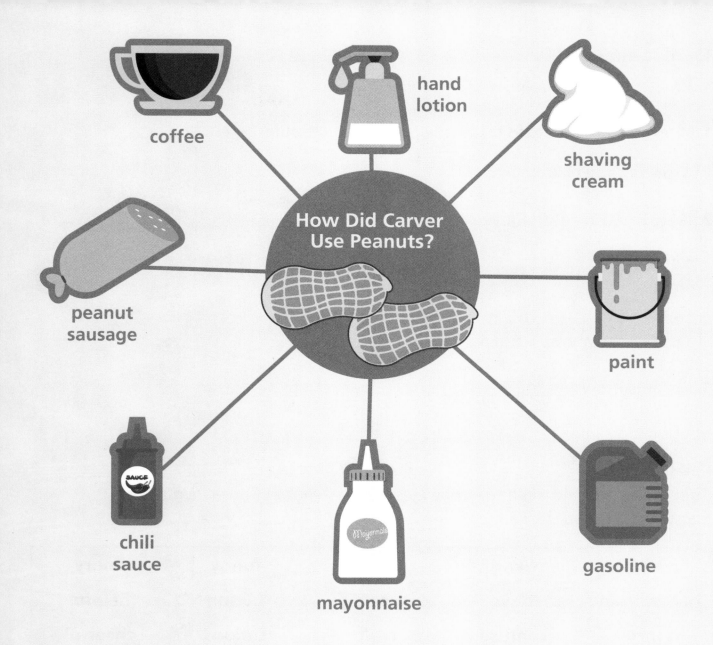

How Did Carver Use Peanuts?

coffee

hand lotion

shaving cream

peanut sausage

paint

chili sauce

mayonnaise

gasoline

How many peanuts does it take to make 1 jar of peanut butter?

= 100 peanuts

Think and Solve

Study the infographic. Answer the questions.

1. It takes 100 peanuts to make one jar of peanut butter.

    True   **False**

2. George Washington Carver was a _____.

    A. scientist

    B. inventor

    C. teacher

    D. all of the above

3. Peanuts grow _____ the ground.

Describe It

Choose five adjectives that describe George Washington Carver. Write them in the spaces.

creative	scientific	smart	funny	angry
hardworking	clever	worried	boring	helpful
lazy	confused	crafty	curious	cheerful

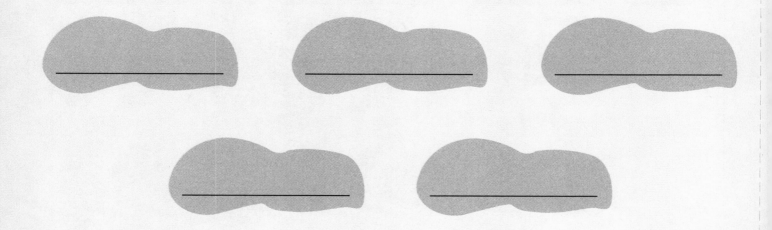

Collect Data

Ask 10 people you know if they like peanut butter. Write their names on the lines. Check a box to show each person's answer.

Yes   No

1. _____ ☐ ☐

2. _____ ☐ ☐

3. _____ ☐ ☐

4. _____ ☐ ☐

5. _____ ☐ ☐

Yes   No

6. _____ ☐ ☐

7. _____ ☐ ☐

8. _____ ☐ ☐

9. _____ ☐ ☐

10. _____ ☐ ☐

Make a Picture Chart

Now, use the data you collected to make a picture chart. Start at the bottom of the peanut butter jar. Color one space for each person who said yes.

How many people out of 10 like peanut butter?

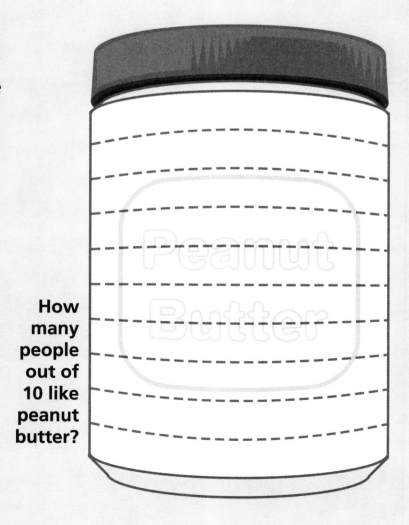

Tugboats on the Move

A tugboat is small but mighty! It can pull or push another boat much larger and heavier than it is. Tugboats help other boats that are in trouble and have lost power.

Some tugboats push a ship. Pushing a ship does not take as much energy. The tugboat can better control the way the other ship moves.

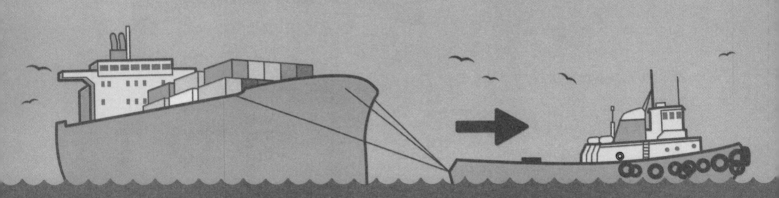

Some tugboats pull a ship. They use their powerful engines to tow the ship.

A tugboat captain must...
⚓ make sure the tugboat is moving in the right direction.
⚓ be on the lookout for other ships in the water.
⚓ take care of the crew.

Think and Solve

Study the infographic. Answer the questions.

1. Tugboats are _____ the boats they help.

   A. bigger than

   B. smaller than

   C. the same size as

2. It takes more energy for a tugboat to push a ship.

   True   **False**

3. A tugboat captain looks for ships that need help and takes care of the

   _____ .

Match It

Draw lines to match words with opposite meanings.

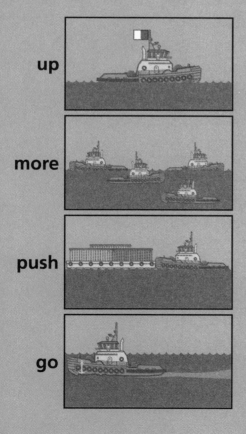

up

more

push

go

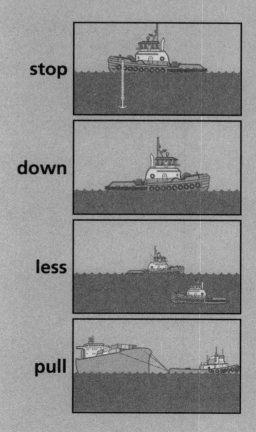

stop

down

less

pull

Super Teeth

Your teeth are very important. Strong, healthy teeth help you chew.
They help you speak clearly. They help you look your best!

You have the POWER!

Squeeze the size of a pea!

Don't rush when you brush!

Floss like a boss!

Make sure to brush every tooth!

Rinse well and spit!

Brush at least twice a day—morning and night!

The Visual Guide to Kindergarten

Eat a lot of these,

not a lot of these!

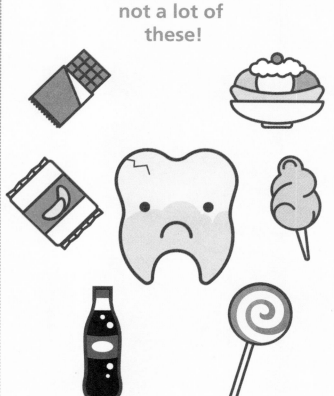

How Long Should You Brush?

Two minutes is...

...about as long as it takes to make a bed.

...the time it takes to sing the song "Bingo" twice.

...about as long as a commercial break on TV.

Think and Solve

Study the infographic. Answer the questions.

1. Brush your teeth at least _____ times each day.

2. What three things do you need to brush and floss your teeth?

_____

_____

_____

3. You should squeeze only a small amount of toothpaste onto your toothbrush.

True   **False**

Show It

Read each item. If it tells about something good for your teeth, draw a smiley face 🙂. If it tells about something bad for your teeth, draw a sad face 🙁.

Eating carrots      Drinking milk

Eating candy   Brushing teeth

Forgetting to floss   Drinking soda

Log It

Keep track of your brushing for one week. Color a sun each time you brush in the morning. Color a moon each time you brush at night. Color the timer each time you brush for at least two minutes.

Day	Morning	Two Minutes?	Night	Two Minutes?
Sunday	☀	⧗	🌙	⧗
Monday	☀	⧗	🌙	⧗
Tuesday	☀	⧗	🌙	⧗
Wednesday	☀	⧗	🌙	⧗
Thursday	☀	⧗	🌙	⧗
Friday	☀	⧗	🌙	⧗
Saturday	☀	⧗	🌙	⧗

Color It

Color Super Tooth. Write something that Super Tooth might say.

Fruit or Veggie?

The market is filled with fresh foods in every color of the rainbow. Some are fruits. Some are vegetables. Can you tell them apart?

Vegetables

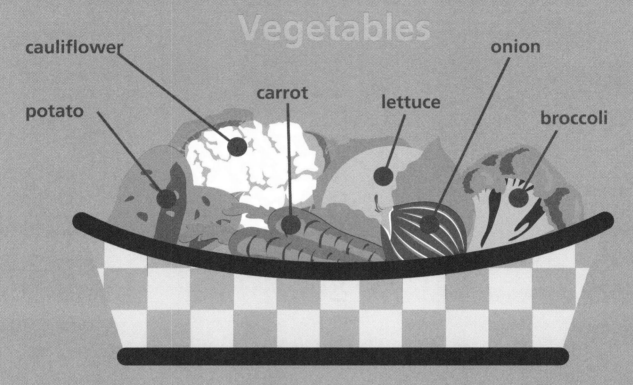

cauliflower

potato

carrot

lettuce

onion

broccoli

Vegetables mostly grow under or close to the ground. They are usually stems, leaves, buds, or roots.

Most Popular

#1
VEGETABLE
potato

#2
VEGETABLE
onion

#3
VEGETABLE
lettuce

A tomato has seeds and grows on a vine — it's a fruit!

Fun Fruit Fact
Tomatoes, cucumbers, green peppers and peas are all fruits because they contain seeds.

165

Fruits

apple

grapes

banana

pear

orange

peach

Fruits have seeds. They usually grow on trees or vines.

Most Popular

#1	#2	#3
FRUIT	**FRUIT**	**FRUIT**
apple	banana	orange

Study the infographic. Answer the questions.

1. A tomato is a fruit.

    True   **False**

2. What is the most popular vegetable?

    A. broccoli

    B. onion

    C. potato

    D. lettuce

3. A cucumber has seeds. It grows on a vine. A cucumber is a _____.

What are your favorite fruits and vegetables? In each list, write 1 beside your most favorite, 2 beside your next favorite, 3 beside your next favorite, and so on.

_____	grapes	_____	broccoli
_____	banana	_____	lettuce
_____	apple	_____	potato
_____	pear	_____	carrot
_____	orange	_____	cauliflower
_____	peach	_____	onion

Cut apart the fruits and vegetables. Glue or tape each one in the correct column on page 169.

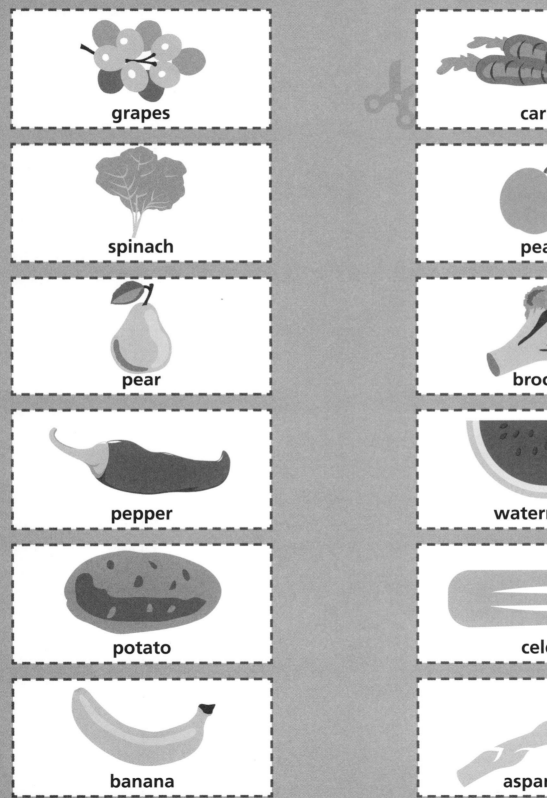

grapes

carrot

spinach

peach

pear

broccoli

pepper

watermelon

potato

celery

banana

asparagus

Fruit
- has seeds
- grows on a vine or tree

Vegetable
- grows in or near the ground
- stems, leaves, buds, or roots

Grown-Up Jobs

What do kids say they want to be when they grow up?

Out of 100 kids ages 2–12...

9 want to be doctors.

8 want to be athletes.

6 want to be dancers.

5 want to be police officers.

4 want to be scientists.

4 want to be musicians.

Which jobs pay the most?

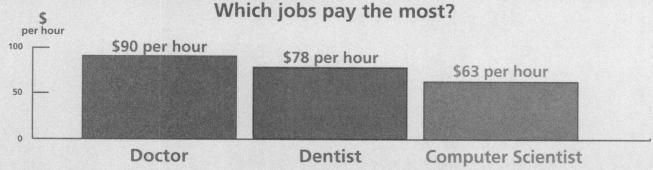

$ per hour

100

50

0

$90 per hour — Doctor

$78 per hour — Dentist

$63 per hour — Computer Scientist

8 want to be teachers.

2 want to be nurses.

4 want to be firefighters.

2 want to be actors.

48 are not sure yet!

How can you reach your goals?

Try new things to find out what you like.
Think about **WORK HARD IN SCHOOL.**
what you **Find adults you respect.**
do well. **Ask them for advice.**

Think and Solve

Study the infographic. Answer the questions.

1. Most kids do not know what they want to be when they grow up.

   True　　　　**False**

2. _____ kids want to be teachers than actors.

   A. Fewer

   B. More

3. A dentist is paid about _____ dollars per hour.

Do the Math

Solve the problems. Use the infographic to help you.

1. How many more kids want to be athletes than nurses?

   _____

2. How many kids in all want to be firefighters, scientists, or musicians?

   _____

3. How many kids in all want to be doctors or teachers? Which number sentence shows the answer?

   A. $9 + 8 = 17$

   B. $17 - 8 = 9$

   C. $9 + 17 = 8$

   D. $17 - 9 = 8$

Match It

Draw lines to match the jobs and pictures.

doctor

scientist

police officer

teacher

musician

Imagine It

What will your grown-up job be? Draw yourself at work in the future. On the lines, write about what you do each day.

Video Games: The Good and the Bad

Do you like to play video games? Are they good or bad for you?

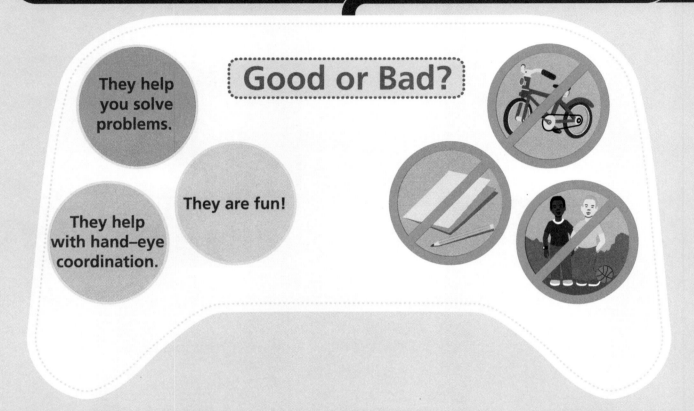

Good or Bad?

They help you solve problems.

They help with hand–eye coordination.

They are fun!

GOOD

Some things about playing video games can be good for you. Playing video games helps you become a quick thinker. Games can make you a better problem solver, too. Video games can help you learn to follow instructions. They can even help with math and reading skills.

BAD

Some things about playing video games can be bad for you. Sometimes, video games are too scary for kids. If you spend all your time playing video games, you won't have time to do other things that make you healthy and happy, like playing outside, talking with friends, and reading books.

A healthy, happy day should look something like this:

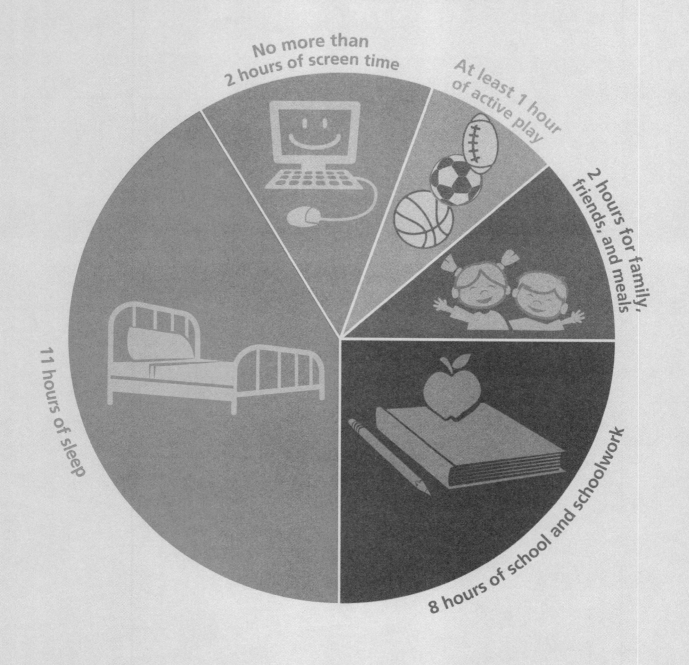

No more than 2 hours of screen time

At least 1 hour of active play

2 hours for family, friends, and meals

8 hours of school and schoolwork

11 hours of sleep

Try this instead of a video game:

- Cook up a new recipe with an adult!
- Paint a picture!
- Play with your pet!
- Build something to solve a problem!
- Play a board game!
- Visit the library!

Log It

There are 24 hours in one day. How do you spend the hours in your day? Choose a day. For each hour, write how you spent your time.

Midnight–1:00 A.M. _____	**Noon–1:00** P.M. _____
1:00–2:00 A.M. _____	**1:00–2:00** P.M. _____
2:00–3:00 A.M. _____	**2:00–3:00** P.M. _____
3:00–4:00 A.M. _____	**3:00–4:00** P.M. _____
4:00–5:00 A.M. _____	**4:00–5:00** P.M. _____
5:00–6:00 A.M. _____	**5:00–6:00** P.M. _____
6:00–7:00 A.M. _____	**6:00–7:00** P.M. _____
7:00–8:00 A.M. _____	**7:00–8:00** P.M. _____
8:00–9:00 A.M. _____	**8:00–9:00** P.M. _____
9:00–10:00 A.M. _____	**9:00–10:00** P.M. _____
10:00–11:00 A.M. _____	**10:00–11:00** P.M. _____
11:00 A.M.–**Noon** _____	**11:00** P.M.–**Midnight** _____

Make a Pie Chart

Use the data from your log to make a pie chart. Each slice of the pie stands for one hour. Color a pie slice to show how you spent each hour. For example, if you were sleeping for nine hours, color nine slices one color. Complete the key to show what each color in your pie chart means.

Key			
Color	Activity	Color	Activity
☐	Sleeping	☐	_____
☐	_____	☐	_____
☐	_____	☐	_____
☐	_____	☐	_____

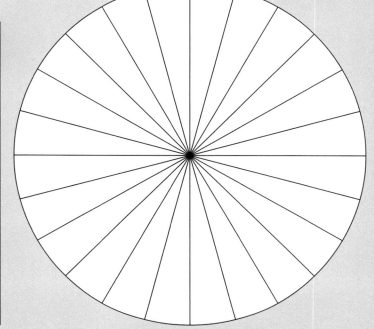

Think and Solve

Study the infographic. Answer the questions.

1. One good thing about video games is _____.

    A. they help you do your homework

    B. they help you sleep better

    C. they can help you learn to solve problems

    D. they help you make new friends

2. How many hours each day should be spent sleeping and doing active play?

_____

3. Video games can keep you from playing outside with friends.

    True   **False**

Answer Key

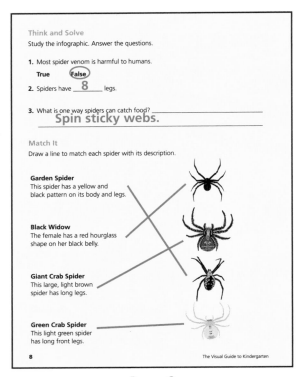

Page 8

Page 11

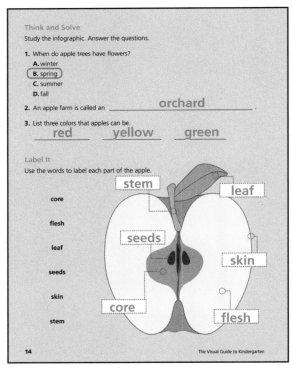

Page 14

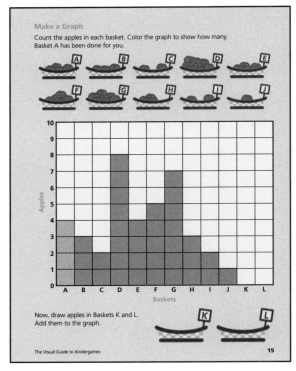

Page 15

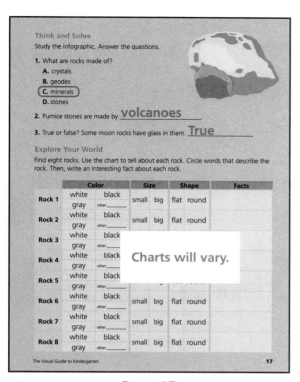

Page 17

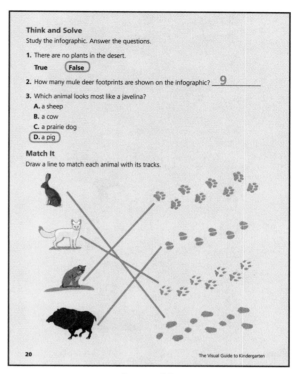

Page 20

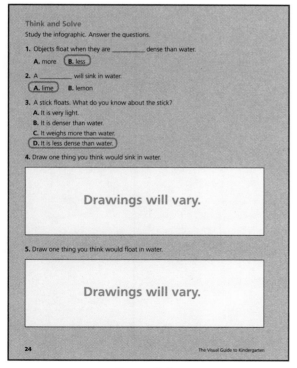

Page 24

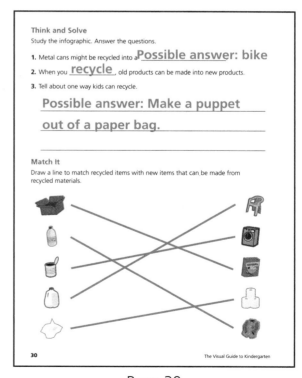

Page 30

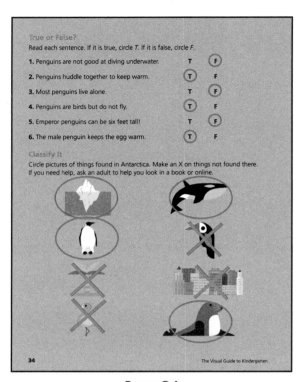

Page 34

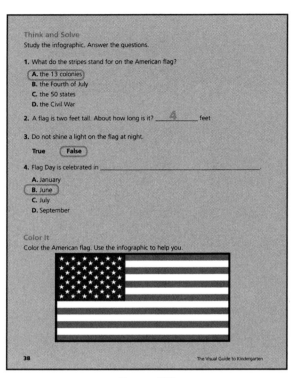

Page 38

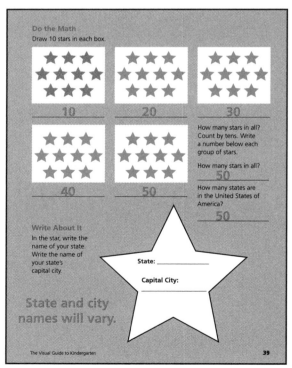

Page 39

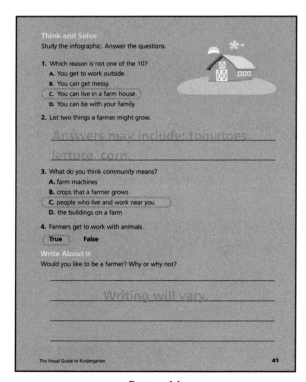

Page 41

Page 45

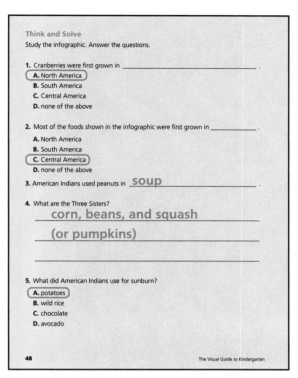

Page 48

Page 49

Page 55

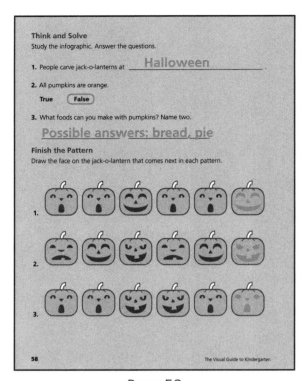

Page 58

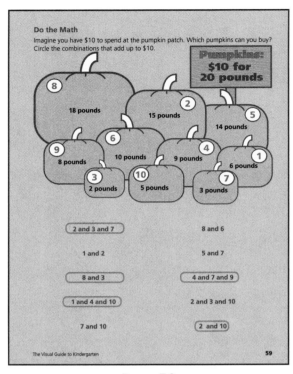

Page 59

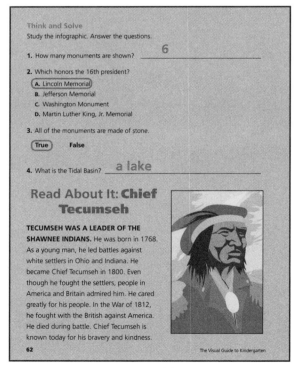

Page 62

Page 66

Page 69

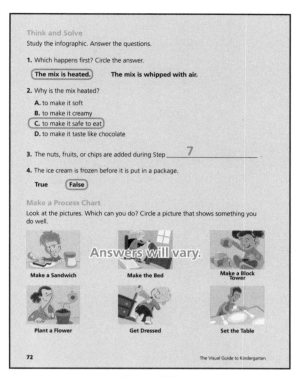

Page 72

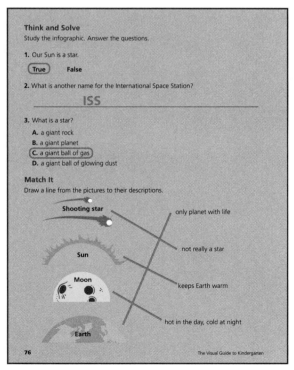

Page 76

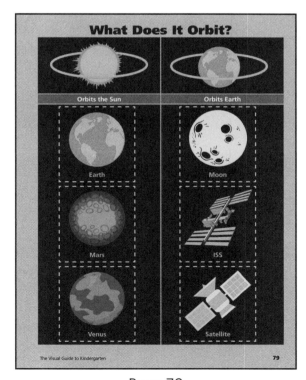

Page 79

Page 82

Think and Solve
Study the infographic. Answer the questions.

1. If you have neighbors close by, you probably live in the

_____ city _____

2. The country is usually a quiet place.

(True)   False

3. Name three things that you might see in the city.

Possible answers: buses, skyscrapers, taxis

4. Would you rather live in the city or in the country? Why?

_____

Answers will vary.

_____

Classify It
Read each group of words. If it describes the city, write *CI*. If it describes the country, write *CO*. If it describes both, write *B*.

CO lots of space   CI a busy, noisy place   CI big buildings

CO grow own food   CO starry nights   B people work there

B people live there   B houses and schools

CO farm animals   CI subways, taxis, buses

Page 83

Compare and Contrast
Look at the list on page 82. Write the words that describe city life in the *City* circle. Write the words that describe country life in the *Country* circle. Write words that describe both in the middle.

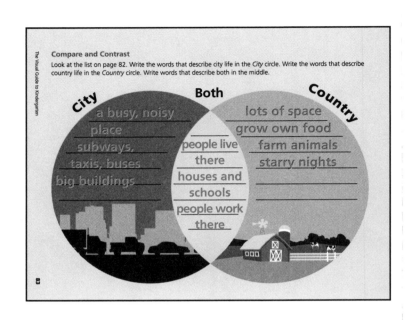

City: a busy, noisy place / subways, taxis, buses / big buildings

Both: people live there / houses and schools / people work there

Country: lots of space / grow own food / farm animals / starry nights

Page 86

Label It
Write the names of the holidays on the continents where they are celebrated.

Children's Day	Chinese New Year
Cinco de Mayo	Homowo Festival
Carnival	Holi
Canada Day	Saint Lucia's Day

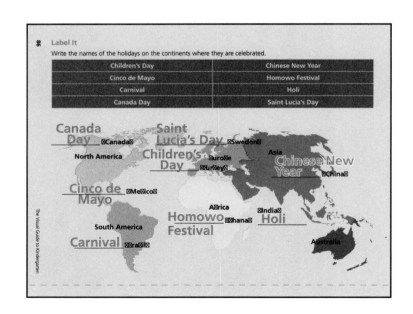

Page 90

Classify It
Look at each picture. If it shows something living, write *L* on the line. If it shows something nonliving, write *N* on the line.

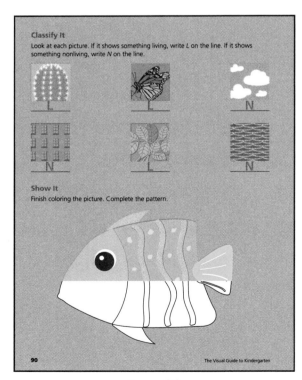

L   L   N

N   L   N

Show It
Finish coloring the picture. Complete the pattern.

Page 91

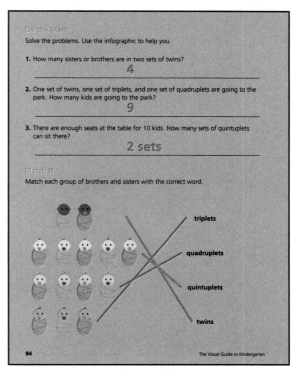

Page 94

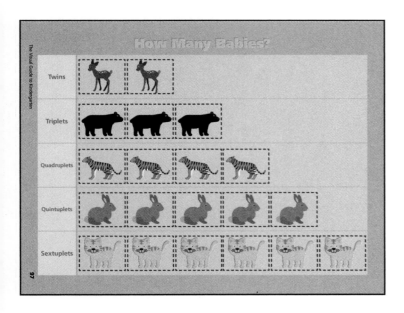

Page 97

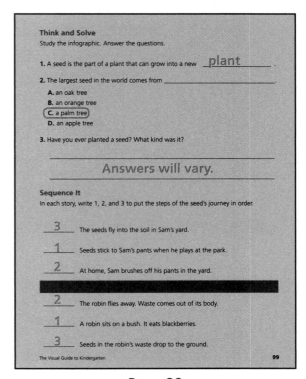

Page 99

Page 102

Think and Solve

Study the infographic. Answer the questions.

1. It takes 20 dimes to make one dollar.

True   (False)

2. Which president is on the front of the quarter?

(A. Washington)   C. Jefferson

B. Lincoln   D. Roosevelt

3. If you have six pennies, then you have ____6____ cents.

Do the Math

Add the value of the coins. Write the total on the line.

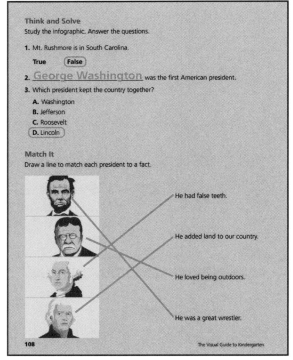

1. __31__ ¢

2. __28__ ¢

3. __15__ ¢

4. __8__ ¢

Page 102

Page 105

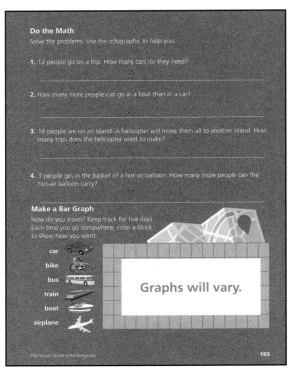

Do the Math

Solve the problems. Use the infographic to help you.

1. 12 people go on a trip. How many cars do they need?

3

2. How many more people can go in a boat than in a car?

4

3. 16 people are on an island. A helicopter will move them all to another island. How many trips does the helicopter need to make?

2

4. 3 people get in the basket of a hot-air balloon. How many more people can the hot-air balloon carry?

7

Make a Bar Graph

How do you travel? Keep track for five days. Each time you go somewhere, color a block to show how you went.

car
bike
bus
train
boat
airplane

Graphs will vary.

The Visual Guide to Kindergarten   105

Page 105

Page 108

Think and Solve

Study the infographic. Answer the questions.

1. Mt. Rushmore is in South Carolina.

True   (False)

2. _George Washington_ was the first American president.

3. Which president kept the country together?

A. Washington
B. Jefferson
C. Roosevelt
(D. Lincoln)

Match It

Draw a line to match each president to a fact.

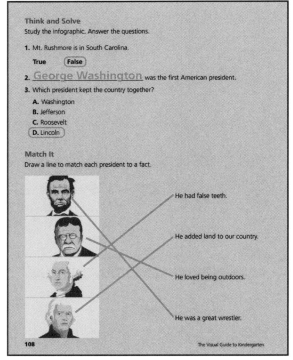

He had false teeth.

He added land to our country.

He loved being outdoors.

He was a great wrestler.

108   The Visual Guide to Kindergarten

Page 108

Page 109

Label It

Write a president's last name under each face on Mt. Rushmore.

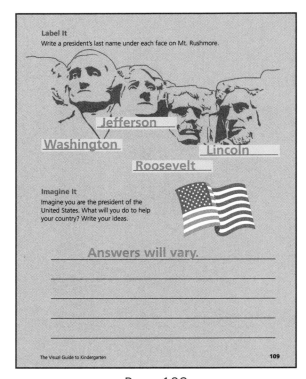

Washington   Jefferson   Lincoln   Roosevelt

Imagine It

Imagine you are the president of the United States. What will you do to help your country? Write your ideas.

Answers will vary.

The Visual Guide to Kindergarten   109

Page 109

186   The Visual Guide to Kindergarten

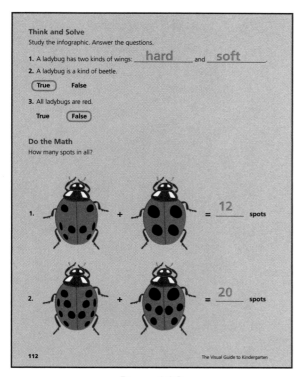

Page 112

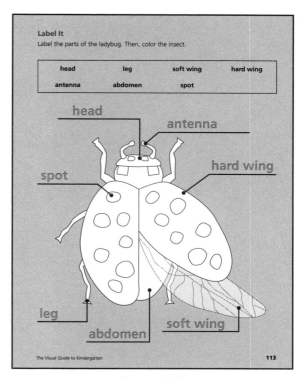

Page 113

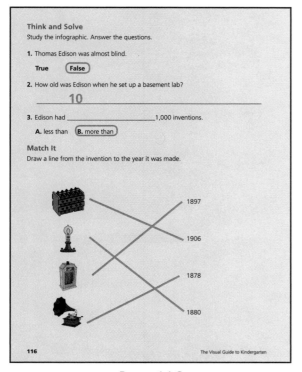

Page 116

Make an Idea Web
Choose five adjectives that describe Thomas Edison. Write them in the web.

| lazy | smart | famous | sad | loud |
| hardworking | tired | great | safe | brave |

smart   famous

hardworking   brave

great

Imagine It
Design a new invention. Draw it in the box. Then, write about it on the lines.

Drawings and descriptions will vary.

The Visual Guide to Kindergarten   117

Page 117

Page 120

Study the infographic. Answer the questions.

1. A killer whale is not a fish.

(True) False

2. The ocean food chain begins with _____

   A. squid
   (B. plankton)
   C. krill
   D. sharks

3. How many different sea creatures are shown in the infographic?

   _____ 9 _____

4. Plankton make their own food.

(True) False

Read About It:
Finding Food in the Forest

PLANTS AND ANIMALS IN THE FOREST ARE PART OF A FOOD CHAIN, too. Plants need sunlight. They use the light to make their own food. Insects and small animals eat the plants. Frogs and rats eat the insects. A snake might eat a frog or a rat. Then, a bigger animal such as a hawk or a fox might eat the snake. In the forest, just like in the ocean, bigger animals need smaller animals in order to survive.

Page 120

Page 123

A Forest Food Chain

Page 123

Page 126

Think and Solve
Study the infographic. Answer the questions.

1. The Liberty Bell is about ___6___ feet wide.
2. The Liberty Bell cracked during a war.

   True (False)

3. Circle which happened first.

   (The Liberty Bell was rung to celebrate the Declaration of Independence.)

   The Liberty Bell cracked for the second time.

4. When was the Liberty Bell hidden?
   1777, during the Revolutionary War

Explore Your World
The Liberty Bell is three feet, or one yard, tall. Ask an adult to help you find a yardstick. Use it to measure things inside and outside. Draw two things you find that are about as tall as the Liberty Bell.

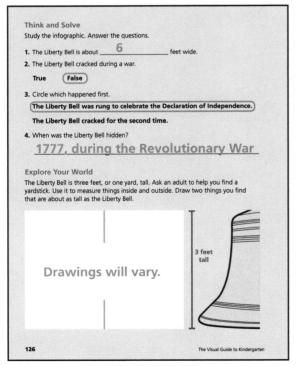

Drawings will vary.

3 feet tall

Page 126

Page 130

Think and Solve
Study the infographic. Answer the questions.

1. Where do children play with nesting dolls?

   A. China
   (B. Russia)
   C. India
   D. United Kingdom

2. Who is the teddy bear named after?

   Teddy Roosevelt

3. Marbles have been around for thousands of years.

   (True) False

4. Which game or toy from around the world would you like to play with? Why?

   Answers will vary.

Sequence It
Write 1, 2, 3, 4, or 5 on each line to put the steps in order.

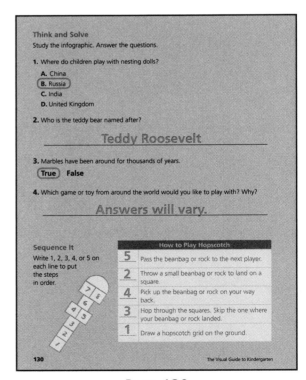

How to Play Hopscotch
5 Pass the beanbag or rock to the next player.
2 Throw a small beanbag or rock to land on a square.
4 Pick up the beanbag or rock on your way back.
3 Hop through the squares. Skip the one where your beanbag or rock landed.
1 Draw a hopscotch grid on the ground.

Page 130

Page 133

Think and Solve

Study the infographic. Answer the questions.

1. Which animal lives the longest?
   A. human
   B. box turtle
   C. macaw
   D. blue whale

2. An opossum and a snake have the same life span.
   True   False

3. How many reptiles are in the infographic? ___3___

Do the Math

Solve the problems. Use the infographic to help you.

1. A duck lives ___3___ years longer than a snake.

2. A dog lives for 14 years. How much longer does a cat live?

   _____ 7 years _____

3. A frog lives twice as long as a duck. How long does a frog live?

   _____ 10 years _____

4. A mouse in the wild lives half as long as an opossum. How long does a mouse live?

   _____ 1 year _____

Page 133

Page 136

Think and Solve

Study the infographic. Answer the questions.

1. What was the name of the Pilgrims' ship?
   A. the *New World*
   B. the *Mayflower*
   C. the *Plymouth*
   D. the *Wampanoag*

2. Before America became a country, it was called the *New World*.
   True   False

3. The American Indians invited the Pilgrims to a feast.
   True   False

4. The Pilgrims began their journey in _____
   A. Plymouth, America
   B. the New World
   C. Plymouth, England
   D. Canada

5. Why did the Pilgrims go to the New World?
   A. to meet the American Indians
   B. to hunt and grow their own food
   C. to look for freedom
   D. to explore the world

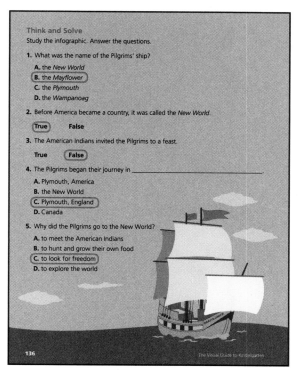

Page 136

Page 137

Match It

Who said it? Read each sentence. Draw a line to the person who might say it.

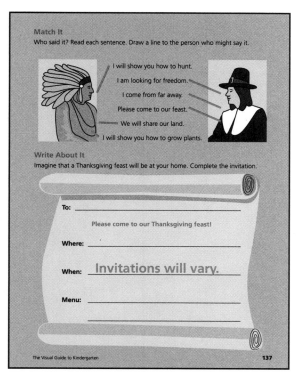

I will show you how to hunt.
I am looking for freedom.
I come from far away.
Please come to our feast.
We will share our land.
I will show you how to grow plants.

Write About It

Imagine that a Thanksgiving feast will be at your home. Complete the invitation.

To: _____

Please come to our Thanksgiving feast!

Where: _____

When: _____ Invitations will vary. _____

Menu: _____

_____

Page 137

Page 144

Think and Solve

Study the infographic. Answer the questions.

1. Name one way the Inuit used animal skins.
   _____ Possible answer: for warm clothing _____

2. An Inuk is not a member of the Inuit people.
   True   False

3. Mukluks are worn on the _____ feet _____

4. Describe an igloo.
   _____ Answers will vary. _____

Match It

Draw a line to match each picture to its meaning.

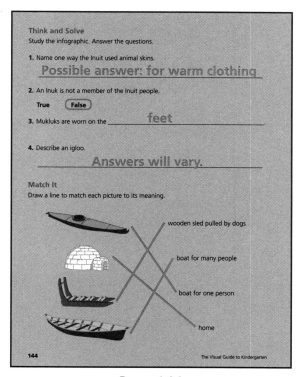

wooden sled pulled by dogs

boat for many people

boat for one person

home

Page 144

Page 145

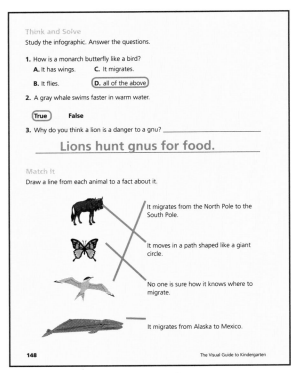

Page 148

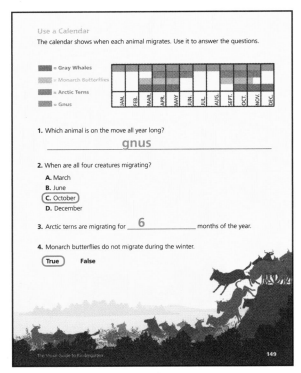

Page 149

Page 152

...

Page 156

Think and Solve
Study the infographic. Answer the questions.

1. It takes 100 peanuts to make one jar of peanut butter.

True   (False)

2. George Washington Carver was a _____.
   A. scientist
   B. inventor
   C. teacher
   (**D.** all of the above)

3. Peanuts grow _under_ the ground.

Describe It
Choose five adjectives that describe George Washington Carver. Write them in the spaces.

creative	scientific	smart	funny	angry
hardworking	clever	worried	boring	helpful
lazy	confused	crafty	curious	cheerful

Answers will vary but may include: creative, scientific, smart, hardworking, clever, helpful, crafty, curious.

156   The Visual Guide to Kindergarten

Page 159

Think and Solve
Study the infographic. Answer the questions.

1. Tugboats are _____ the boats they help.
   A. bigger than
   (**B.** smaller than)
   C. the same size as

2. It takes more energy for a tugboat to push a ship.

True   (False)

3. A tugboat captain looks for ships that need help and takes care of the
   crew _____

Match It
Draw lines to match words with opposite meanings.

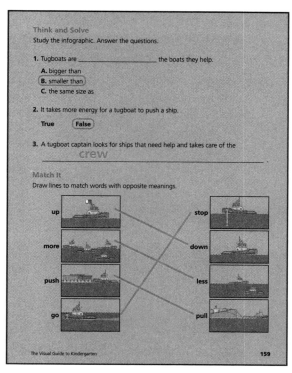

up — stop
more — down
push — less
go — pull

The Visual Guide to Kindergarten   159

Page 162

Think and Solve
Study the infographic. Answer the questions.

1. Brush your teeth at least __2__ times each day.

2. What three things do you need to brush and floss your teeth?
   toothbrush
   toothpaste
   floss

3. You should squeeze only a small amount of toothpaste onto your toothbrush.

(True)   False

Show It
Read each item. If it tells about something good for your teeth, draw a smiley face ☺. If it tells about something bad for your teeth, draw a sad face ☹.

Eating carrots ☺   Drinking milk ☺

Eating candy ☹   Brushing teeth ☺

Forgetting to floss ☹   Drinking soda ☹

162   The Visual Guide to Kindergarten

Page 166

Study the infographic. Answer the questions.

1. A tomato is a fruit.

(True)   False

2. What is the most popular vegetable?
   A. broccoli
   B. onion
   (**C.** potato)
   D. lettuce

3. A cucumber has seeds. It grows on a vine. A cucumber is a _fruit_ _____

What are your favorite fruits and vegetables? In each list, write 1 beside your most favorite, 2 beside your next favorite, 3 beside your next favorite, and so on.

_____ grapes   _____ broccoli
_____ banana   _____ lettuce
_____ apple   _____ potato
_____ pear   _____ carrot
_____ orange   _____ cauliflower
_____ peach   _____ onion

Rankings will vary.

166   The Visual Guide to Kindergarten

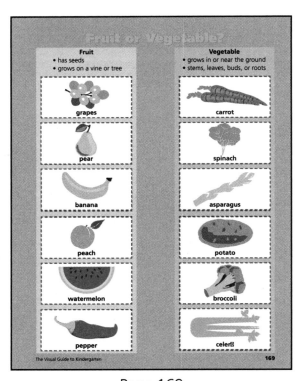

Page 169

Page 172

Think and Solve

Study the infographic. Answer the questions.

1. Most kids do not know what they want to be when they grow up.

   (True)   False

2. _____ kids want to be teachers than actors.

   A. Fewer
   (B. More)

3. A dentist is paid about ___78___ dollars per hour.

Do the Math

Solve the problems. Use the infographic to help you.

1. How many more kids want to be athletes than nurses?

   _____ 6 _____

2. How many kids in all want to be firefighters, scientists, or musicians?

   _____ 12 _____

3. How many kids in all want to be doctors or teachers? Which number sentence shows the answer?

   (A. 9 + 8 = 17)
   B. 17 − 8 = 9
   C. 9 + 17 = 8
   D. 17 − 9 = 8

172   The Visual Guide to Kindergarten

Page 172

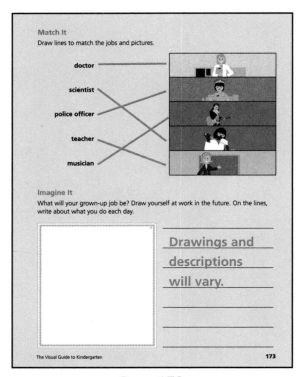

Page 173

Page 177

Make a Pie Chart

Use the data from your log to make a pie chart. Each slice of the pie stands for one hour. Color a pie slice to show how you spent each hour. For example, if you were sleeping for nine hours, color nine slices one color. Complete the key to show what each color in your pie chart means.

Key			
Color	Activity	Color	Activity
☐	Sleeping	☐	____
☐	____	☐	____
☐	____	☐	____
☐	____	☐	____

Think and Solve

Study the infographic. Answer the questions.

1. One good thing about video games is _____.

   A. they help you do your homework
   B. they help you sleep better
   (C. they can help you learn to solve problems)
   D. they help you make new friends

2. How many hours each day should be spent sleeping and doing active play?

   _____ 12 _____

3. Video games can keep you from playing outside with friends.

   (True)   False

The Visual Guide to Kindergarten   177

Page 177

192   The Visual Guide to Kindergarten